Joyce

Joyce

Ian Pindar

HAUS PUBLISHING · LONDON

FOR MY PARENTS

The mockery of it, he said gaily. Your
absurd name, an ancient Greek.
Ulysses

First published in Great Britain in 2004 by
Haus Publishing Limited
32 Store Street
London WC1E 7BS

Copyright © Ian Pindar, 2004

The moral right of the author has been asserted

A CIP catalogue record for this book
is available from the British Library

ISBN 1-904341-58-6

Typeset by Lobster
Printed and bound by Graphicom in Vicenza, Italy

Front cover: photograph of James Joyce, © courtesy of Topham Picturepoint
Back cover: photograph of James Joyce, © courtesy of AKG-Images

Contents

Introduction

Asked by a French journalist whether he was English, James Joyce's friend and colleague Samuel Beckett replied: '*Au contraire.*' Though Joyce himself was bitterly critical of his native Ireland, as Ian Pindar shows in this lucid, informative study, it is not out of the question that he might have replied in much the same way. It is easy to mistake Irish writers for English ones, since most of them write in the English language – but only because the language was foisted upon them by the English in the first place. Rather as English colonialists had helped suppress the Irish language, so Joyce's *Finnegans Wake* returns the compliment by using English with such dazzling virtuosity that it falls apart at the seams. The *Daily Express* of the day commented darkly that reading the book was rather like taking a trip into the alien territory of Soviet Russia.

Even so, when Irish writers like Oscar Wilde, George Bernard Shaw, W B Yeats or James Joyce use the language even more brilliantly and resourcefully than the English themselves, they are usually granted honorary places in the English literary canon, despite the fact that Joyce was no more English than Madonna or Nelson Mandela. The English, like most other nations, are adept at picking up foreigners who make good, and dropping those who do not. Oscar Wilde was finally to suffer the latter fate. When the Irish actor Richard Harris won an award for one of his films, some English newspapers carried the headline ENGLISH ACTOR HONOURED. When he was involved in a punch-up in a pub, the headlines read IRISH ACTOR IN BAR BRAWL.

Joyce, as this book makes clear, was picked up only belatedly by the critics and academics and would no doubt be astonished to know that he is now the linchpin of a major industry in his native land, not quite as big as Guinness, but for some of his devotees every bit as intoxicating. A silhouette of the author in jaunty posture, complete with hat and stick, is today an instantly recognizable logo in the Ireland which once drove him into exile as a Satanic blasphemer. This most elusive, esoteric of men is now public property. There are James Joyce posters, breakfasts and pub crawls, while scholars flock to Dublin from Japan or Peru to debate the meaning of his work. For Irish writers, he has proved an impossibly hard act to follow, casting his long, chilling shadow over their computers. If history is a nightmare from which Stephen Dedalus of *Ulysses* is trying to awaken, *Ulysses* is the nightmare from which Ireland is trying to awaken. Joyce has been one of the country's major exports. While other nations export bazookas or bananas, Ireland has traditionally traded in culture, from Joyce and the Chieftains to *Riverdance* and U2.

With characteristic arrogance, Joyce expected his readers to spend as much time reading his great novel *Finnegans Wake* as he himself had spent writing it; and some of his more scholarly readers seem to have taken him at his word. The man who in his own day was a scrounger, loafer, rebel, toper, plagiarist and small-time language teacher is now literary big business. I once took part in a conference in a small town in China at which an elderly Chinese scholar who had produced a Chinese version of *Ulysses* spent a whole hour explaining how he had translated a single word of the novel into the language. It has been suggested that the book needs first to be translated into English. I have also taken part in a conference entitled 'Californian Joyce', where the lean, tanned, granola-eating academics of San Diego and Santa Barbara claimed this myopic, obscenity-spouting Dubliner as their own.

That Joyce wrote English as a non-Englishman is not irrelevant to his achievement. Many of the most eminent names in modern English letters – from Henry James, Joseph Conrad and T S Eliot to Ezra Pound, Doris Lessing and Salman Rushdie – were semi-outsiders to English culture, with one foot in and one foot out of it. To see a language and culture as both strange and intimate is a time-honoured way of unlocking its deepest resources. Joyce remarked to his brother that it was his freedom from English convention which lay at the source of his talent; and what he meant by this, perhaps, was that he felt less constrained by an established canon and tradition than many a native artist. He was able to chance his arm, cobble things together, make them up as he went along. He could turn his lack of a stable cultural tradition to artistic advantage, creating something startlingly new. *Ulysses* appeared in the same year as the founding of the Irish Free State, and that, too, was an original creation, the first post-colonial nation-state of the twentieth century. Like Joyce, it lacked an established model and would find itself having to cobble things together and make them up as it went along.

Like Eliot and Pound, then, Joyce was free to pick and mix his cultures. Much of the great 'English' writing of the twentieth century was produced by men and women who felt uprooted and displaced – émigrés, dissenters and spiritual vagrants who wandered from country to country, setting up home with their art. Joyce was one of the most prominent of this number – yet he was also the one who kept the channels of communication with his native country most open. Getting out of Ireland, not least since the Great Famine, was nothing new. Indeed, exile is one of the most typical of all Irish experiences. Nothing is more native to the country than fleeing it as fast as you can – despite the fact that the Almighty in His wisdom has placed the mountains in the country around the coasts rather than in the centre, as though in a desperate attempt to keep the population from leaving.

Joyce was raised on an island which already had far more people living off it than living on it. It was the nation who was not at home, not just the writer. And just as the sons and daughters of small farmers who left for Boston and Birmingham wrote their letters home, so Joyce wrote home in the form of his fiction. He was one of the first generation of artists to live in a world in which places were becoming more and more interchangeable, as the early twentieth century witnessed the first stirrings of what we now call globalization. The last words of *Ulysses* are not *yes I said yes I will Yes* but *Trieste-Zurich-Paris, 1914–1921*. Joyce hailed from the down-at-heel capital city of a country he described as *an afterthought of Europe*, but through his art he shifted it to the centre of the map. He was a cosmopolitan type through and through, a man of the world in every sense of the phrase. Those from small nations often are. It is the superpowers who are the most provincial.

Yet cosmopolitanism, too, was nothing new in Ireland. It was, in fact, quite literally very old. The Middle Ages witnessed an intense traffic between Ireland and Europe, though the merchandise in question was not so much corn or wine but monks and missionaries. In trudging between Paris, Zurich and Trieste, Joyce is keeping faith with a tradition in which medieval Ireland supplied the Continent with many of its philosophers and intellectuals, establishing Irish colleges from Rome to Salamanca. It is no accident that Joyce's nation is today far more enthusiastic about the European Union than its geographical neighbour.

Joyce stands out from his great literary contemporaries in three chief ways. For one thing, he was a man who, to use his own sardonic self-description, had a mind like a grocer. Part of what he meant by this, perhaps (since grocers stack items neatly upon shelves), was that his mind was an obsessively systematizing one. Like Beckett, he is fascinated by the endless permutations you can pluck out of the same few elements, the different ways you can stack the same bits and pieces. But he probably also meant – since grocers are not usually thought of as aloof, ivory-tower types – that he had an astonishingly down-to-earth sort of imagination.

Joyce is magnificently mundane. No writer of his stature has been so enthralled by the sheer unmitigated drabness of daily life – not least daily life in a wretchedly poor, economically stagnant colony. The Ireland he sprang from was for the most part a barren, impoverished, inward-looking place, more of a Third World than a First World nation, and Joyce's reverence for the lowly, for all his verbal exuberance, is among other things a way of keeping faith with his roots. In the deepest sense of the word, it is a political act.

Like many of the Irish, he is a great debunker of the pompous and high-minded. He would doubtless have commended a book like this, which sets out the vital facts of his life and work in the most accessible, companionable form. Ireland, however, was also laced with wit, anecdote, debunkery, pugnacious satire and carnivalesque humour; and it is hard to see how, without this heritage as well, Joyce's work would have been remotely possible. If the Dublin of *Ulysses* is static and inert – nobody, for example, seems to do much work – it is also strangely buoyant and vibrant. What gives it these qualities above all is the language of the book, which takes the unredeemed stuff of everyday experience and transforms it into the imperishable truth of art. It is not the first time in Ireland that language is used to transfigure a situation which can be changed in no other way.

The first way in which Joyce stands out, then, is in his extraordinary combination of the esoteric and the everyday. If he is a high priest of art, formidably difficult and perversely obscure, his writing is also laced with popular culture and loud with the voices of the common people. This then leads us to the second way in which he is different from Pound, Yeats, Eliot, D H Lawrence and a number of his Modernist colleagues. It is that whereas many of them held extreme right-wing views, Joyce is remarkable for his liberal decency and enlightened tolerance. Why else would he make the modern Ulysses a foreign Jew? While other distinguished writers were championing eugenics for the poor, vilifying women, praising Mussolini or indulging in anti-Semitic rant, Joyce spoke up bravely and unfashionably for what we might roughly call social democratic values. He was a jester, not a hater, a pluralist rather than an elitist, a man who practised in his art a kind of joyful cosmic acceptance rather than a jealous exclusion. *Finnegans Wake*, which broke upon the world along with the Second World War, has been described as a great anti-fascist novel – not because it has much to say about fascism, but because its mongrelized mix of styles and languages is the opposite of the creed of racial purity which sent so many to their deaths.

Thirdly, and relatedly, Joyce is almost alone in the ranks of the great Modernist writers of twentieth-century Europe in being comic rather than tragic in his outlook. Until about 1880, it was unacceptable for a novelist to end his or her book unhappily; from then onward, it became almost compulsory to do so. But Joyce is comic because he does not believe in endings in the first place. As Ian Pindar points out, he learned from the Italian philosopher Bruno that everything is recycled, everything returns in a slightly varied version of itself, nothing in the great cosmic and historical circuits can be absolutely lost. If *Finnegans Wake* has its tail in its mouth, so for Joyce does the *neverchanging everchanging* universe itself. And since absolute loss is the mark of tragedy rather than comedy, Joyce is comic in a sense which cuts deeper than just being very funny. Which, of course, he is as well, as the reader new to this prodigious artist is just about to discover.

TERRY EAGLETON

From Baby Tuckoo to Sunny Jim

My father had an extraordinary affection for me, wrote James Joyce in 1932. *He was the silliest man I ever knew and yet cruelly shrewd . . . I was very fond of him always, being a sinner myself, and even liked his faults. Hundreds of pages and scores of characters in my books came from him.*[1]

John Stanislaus Joyce (1849–1931) was 'a dapper little man, with military moustache, who sported an eyeglass and cane, and wore spats'.[2] Talented but reckless, he lived beyond his means and frittered away his inheritance until he was forced to take a full-time job. In 1880, through political connections, he obtained the position of Collector of Rates. This sent him into Dublin, where he very soon knew everyone's business, and his tales of Dublin characters and stories from his days as a rate collector would eventually find their way into his son's fiction. To entertain friends and family, John Joyce would imitate the Dubliners he met on his rounds and Joyce inherited this talent for mimicry, putting it to early use in

Tall tales: John Joyce

Kisses: May Joyce

a school play when he took off one of the masters. As one friend observed, 'Joyce could have been a great actor.'[3]

John Joyce was a kind and affectionate man, verging on the sentimental. He nicknamed his eldest son 'Baby Tuckoo' and would tell him about a mythical cow that came down from the mountain: *Once upon a time and a very good time it was there was a moocow coming down along the road and this moocow that was coming down along the road met a nicens little boy named baby tuckoo . . .* [4] Joyce's father makes regular appearances in his son's work. He is disguised as an uncle in the short stories 'The Sisters' (1904) and 'Araby' (1905) and his fall in a Dublin bar inspired 'Grace' (1905). There is even something of him in Joyce's last great creation, Humphrey Chimpden Earwicker. More overtly, in *A Portrait of the Artist as a Young Man* (1916) and *Ulysses* (1922), John Joyce is the model for Simon Dedalus, who is summed up by his son, Stephen, as *A medical student, an oarsman, a tenor, an amateur actor, a shouting politician, a small landlord, a small investor, a drinker, a good fellow, a storyteller, somebody's secretary, something in a distillery, a tax-gatherer, a bankrupt and at present a praiser of his own past.*[5]

John Joyce was, in short, a Dublin 'character'. The city boasted more than its fair share of brilliant failures; minor celebrities with quick tongues and ready wits who could be depended upon to tell a tall tale down the pub. And James Joyce? He was destined, it seemed, to become a 'character' too. He inherited his father's eloquence and wit, but also his oaths and obscenities; his jokes and put-downs and his comic and bawdy songs, but also the English and Irish ballads which he sang so beautifully with his father's *quaint accent and phrasing*.[6]

Joyce was a good listener and was blessed with an extraordinary memory. A 'blotting-paper memory', one friend called it.[7] He could remember a song after hearing it only once and, as well as being steeped in the language of the Bible and the Roman Catholic liturgy, he could quote long passages of poetry and prose without recourse to the printed word. By the time he had finished university, he was, in effect, a walking library. And if he sometimes worried that he lacked imagination, he could always depend upon his prodigious powers of recall. After all, as he once confided to a friend, *Imagination is memory*.[8]

Joyce's mother, Mary Jane or 'May' (1859–1903), 'a frail, sad-faced, and gentle lady', was extremely fond of her eldest child and, according to one school friend, Joyce 'worshipped' her.[9] After James came Margaret Alice ('Poppie') in January 1884 and in December that same year, John Stanislaus ('Stannie'); then Charles Patrick (1886), George Alfred (1887), Eileen Isabel Mary Xavier Brigid (1889), Mary

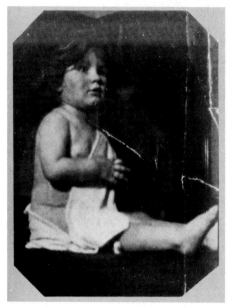

Baby Tuckoo

Kathleen (1890), Eva Mary (1891), Florence Elizabeth (1892) and finally Mabel Josephine Anne ('Baby') in 1893. The exhausting business of looking after her husband and giving birth to so many children ruined May's health and contributed to her early death. She came from Leitrim, a rural province of Connacht in the west of Ireland, and John Joyce, who hailed from Cork City in the southern province of Munster, was always a little snobbish about her family.

May and John were living at 41 Brighton Square, West Rathgar, a Dublin suburb, when their first surviving child James Augustine Joyce was born on 2 February 1882. All of Ireland at that time was still under British rule and three months after Joyce's birth an event occurred in Dublin that was to poison Anglo-Irish relations for years to come, with serious repercussions for the Home Rule movement.

The Home Rule movement (founded in 1870) sought to give Ireland its own law-making body responsible for home affairs. Two Home Rule bills were defeated, but in 1914 a third was passed, only to be put off until after the War. In 1920 a revised act was passed providing separate parliaments for northern and southern Ireland. This was accepted by the north, but rejected by the south, which in 1922 (the year *Ulysses* was published) became completely self-governing as the Irish Free State.

On 6 May 1882 Gladstone's nephew Lord Frederick Cavendish, the Chief Secretary for Ireland, and T H Burke, an Irish Catholic undersecretary, were stabbed to death near the Wellington monument in Dublin's Phoenix Park. Their murderers belonged to the Invincibles, a militant group formed a year before with the intention of assassinating leading British figures. As Joyce later observed, political assassination was just one of the methods employed by Irish revolutionaries to awaken the conscience of Liberal England, along with bombings, boycotts, armed revolts and eloquence.[10] He refers to the murders in *Ulysses* and the central event in his last book *Finnegans Wake* (1939) is an unspecified crime in Phoenix Park.

Joyce was a slim, well-behaved child of such a contented disposition he was nicknamed 'Sunny Jim' and in September 1888 the six year old entered Clongowes Wood College, a fashionable Jesuit school for boys near Sallins, County Kildare. At his confirmation he took the saint's name 'Aloysius' after St Aloysius Gonzaga (1568–91), the patron saint of youth, who died aged 23 while tending to plague victims. Aloysius did not fear dying from the plague, but as Joyce's alter ego Stephen recalls in *A Portrait*, the saint *would not suffer his mother to kiss him as he feared the contact of her sex.*[12] Stephen suffers from a similar anxiety (*His mother kissed him. Was that right?*) and at Clongowes the boys tease him: *Tell us, Dedalus, do you kiss your mother before you go to bed?*[13] Joyce was never to resolve the question of how he should act towards his mother.

In *A Portrait of the Artist as a Young Man* Joyce gives the impression he was constantly miserable at Clongowes; and once, it is true, he was unfairly punished when someone broke his glasses (Father James Daly – Father Dolan in *A Portrait* – assumed it was a ruse to avoid lessons).[14] A highly developed sense of injustice led the seven year old to object to the rector. Father John Conmee accepted his account of the event and Joyce was vindicated, although the school's Punishment Book also reveals he was given the pandybat (a leather strap reinforced with whalebone)

W E Gladstone (1809–98) was Liberal Prime Minister from 1868 to 1874, then again from 1880 to 1886 and 1892 to 1894. Joyce complained of Gladstone's inconstancy and the *elastic quality* of his liberalism: *Gladstone was, in a word, a politician.*[11]

The Society of Jesus was founded in 1540 by the Spaniard Ignatius of Loyola to convert the heathen overseas. The Jesuits see it as their mission to conquer the world for Christ. They place great emphasis on education and it was not by accident that Joyce was a deeply learned man with knowledge of a wide variety of subjects.

for forgetting to bring a book to class, for wearing his boots in the living quarters and for 'vulgar language'.[15] Nevertheless, Joyce received a good education at Clongowes and the Jesuits taught him to improve and to organize his exceptional memory. He loved encyclopedias, catalogues and inventories, keys and plans and long lists of paraphernalia. In later life his notebooks were full of lists and questions reminiscent of the catechisms he had been taught at school.

Joyce was too young to remember what he later called *the savage assassination in the Phoenix Park*, but at the age of nine he was deeply affected by the *moral assassination of Parnell*.[16] The gifted politician Charles Stewart Parnell (1846–91) had led the Irish Parliamentary Party (IPP) into a coalition with Gladstone's Liberal Party in exchange for the Prime Minister's guarantee that he was committed to Home Rule for Ireland. The result was the first Home Rule Bill (1886). Although it was defeated (as was a second in 1893), Parnell's reputation soared in Ireland where he was compared to Moses leading his people to the Promised Land. But there was trouble ahead.

In April 1887 *The Times* of London published a letter, apparently in Parnell's handwriting, condoning the Phoenix Park Murders. Parnell protested his innocence and eventually a man named Richard Pigott was unmasked as the forger of the letter. A crucial element in the case was his misspelling of the word 'hesitancy', a detail Joyce was to remember in *Finnegans Wake*. Disgraced, Pigott committed suicide and the scandal was at an end, though another was brewing.

This lovely land that always sent
Her writers and artists to banishment
And in a spirit of Irish fun
Betrayed her own leaders, one by one.
'Twas Irish humour, wet and dry,
Flung quicklime into Parnell's eye . . .
from 'Gas from a Burner' (1912)[17]

On 2 December 1889 Captain William Henry O'Shea filed a petition for divorce from his wife Katherine ('Kitty') on the grounds that for ten years she had been having an adulterous relationship with none other than Parnell. The divorce was granted without contest in November 1890 and Parnell became a hunted man. As Simon Dedalus puts it in *A Portrait*: *When he was down they turned on him to betray him and rend him like rats in a sewer.*[18] The IPP was split by the scandal, with Parnell's second-in-command Tim Healy pressuring him to resign. Gladstone declared he would not continue his alliance with the IPP if Parnell remained leader. And for good measure, Ireland's Catholic bishops weighed in against Parnell's immoral conduct. A broken man, Parnell resigned. He died 14 weeks after marrying Kitty O'Shea. The day he died, 6 October 1891, is commemorated as 'Ivy Day' by his supporters; hence the title of Joyce's short story 'Ivy Day in the Committee Room' (1905), which depicts the mood of failure and recrimination surrounding Parnell's death.

Joyce's father and his friends were Parnellites and they instilled in him a view of the Chief as a tragic hero. The poem Joyce wrote aged nine, 'Et Tu, Healy', portrays Parnell as Julius Caesar betrayed by his second-in-command and the tragedy of Ireland's *Uncrowned King* resonates throughout Joyce's fiction.[19] In *A Portrait* he re-creates Christmas dinner in 1891, when his outraged governess left the table in disgust at the blasphemous opinions of John Joyce and his Parnellite friends. *O, he'll remember all this when he grows up*, she declares, *the language he heard against God and religion and priests in his own home.*[20] And so he did, for Joyce agreed wholeheartedly with his father (whose anticlericalism increased after the fall of Parnell) that the Irish were *A priestridden Godforsaken race!*[21]

The fall of Parnell was an early initiation into the complex world of Irish politics and Joyce's youthful indignation was levelled less at the British Empire than at the Irish themselves. At times all he could see was weakness, irresolution, faint-heartedness and duplicity, coupled with an ignorant, slavish and superstitious submission to the Catholic Church. *No honourable and sincere man*, Stephen tells his friends in *A Portrait, has given up to you his life and his youth and his affections from the days of Tone to those of Parnell but you sold him to the enemy or failed him in need or reviled him and left him for another. And you invite me to be one of you. I'd see you damned first.*[22] Joyce was to fall back on this defiant assessment of his countrymen many times in his life. It motivated him to abandon his homeland for ever and was a crucial component in his view of himself as an Irish genius spurned by Ireland. Later he could say about one Dublin friend who had disappointed him: *He was Irish, that is to say, he was false to me.*[23]

All was not well in the Joyce household in the year of Parnell's death. John Joyce could no longer afford his son's school fees and withdrew him from Clongowes Wood College. It came as something of a relief to Joyce, although part of him was ashamed at this sudden fall from grace. In 1891 John Joyce's position as Collector of Rates was abolished and he was forced to retire, aged 42, on a far from adequate pension. Joyce's father was never again to have a regular job and his profligate ways and fondness for a tipple only contributed to the family's straitened circumstances. As Joyce was to observe much later: *My home was simply a middle-class affair ruined by spendthrift habits which I have inherited.*[24]

In 1893 the Joyces moved to a *bare cheerless house* at 14 Fitzgibbon Street off Mountjoy Square, Dublin.[25] John Joyce sat down with his eldest son and attempted to explain the situation. Joyce *became slowly aware that his father had enemies and that some fight was going to take place. He felt too that he was being enlisted for the fight, that some duty was being laid upon his shoulders.*[26] This sense of life as a constant battle never left him.

The nationalist Theobald Wolfe Tone (1763–98) founded the United Irishmen (which wanted Irish independence from Britain) and raised support in America and France. He was captured during the 1789 Rebellion and committed suicide.

Dublin: *Grafton Street gay with housed awnings lured his senses* (*Ulysses*)

Around this time he was sent to the Christian Brothers' school on North Richmond Street, but it was not as fashionable as Clongowes and Joyce has left no record of this period in his life. On the other hand, *Dublin was a new and complex sensation.*[27] He was now *in the midst of a new scene, every event and figure of which affected him intimately, disheartened him or allured him.*[28]

By chance John Joyce bumped into Father Conmee, who was now the prefect of studies at Belvedere College, a Jesuit boys' day school on Denmark Street in north-east Dublin. Remembering young James as an extremely able pupil, Conmee arranged for him to enter Belvedere free of charge in April 1893. It was an extraordinary stroke of luck, although, in the social hierarchy of Belvedere, Joyce was acutely aware of his *equivocal position* as a 'free boy' whose parents paid no fees.[29]

A word frequently used of Joyce at this time is 'aloof'. One school friend remembered him as 'a tall slight stripling with flashing teeth – white as a hound's – pale blue eyes that sometimes had an icy look, and mobile sensitive mouth. He was fond of throwing back his head as he walked, and his mood alternated between cold, slightly haughty, aloofness and sudden boisterous merriment.'[30] Those cold blue eyes seemed to look through people 'to a distant object beyond'.[31] Joyce was unusually mature for his age and, like his father, had firm opinions on almost everything. Another friend was struck by the way Joyce 'talked as a formed person talking to one whom he suspected of being unformed'.[32] He affected a supercilious air and an appearance of being unshockable, for as one friend observed, 'it took a good deal to disturb Joyce's equanimity'.[33]

At Belvedere Joyce did well in his studies and gained a high opinion of himself, a view supported by his father, who, despite mounting debts, scraped together sufficient funds to buy the strange, foreign books his son requested. John Joyce was convinced his eldest son was destined for great things, and this made Sunny Jim rather arrogant. He was treated differently to the rest of the family, as if all of their hopes depended on him. This was gratifying, but it was also a burden he would shrug off when the time came. Although fond of his family, Joyce was not prepared to sacrifice his talents in its support.

The Greek poet Homer (c.800 BC) is traditionally regarded as the author of the *Iliad* and the *Odyssey*, though these epic poems were not written down until 600 BC. Born in Smyrna, Homer voyaged to many parts of Greece (including Ithaca), suffered poverty, blindness and lack of appreciation and died on Ios.

At the age of 12 Joyce read Charles Lamb's *The Adventures of Ulysses* (1808) – *Homer's story told in simple English much abbreviated*.[34] He was fascinated by Ulysses and Lamb's depiction of him probably informed Joyce's own self-image: 'a brave man struggling with adversity; by a wise use of events, and with an inimitable presence of mind under difficulties, forcing out a way for himself through the severest trials to which human life can be exposed; with enemies natural and preternatural surrounding him on all sides.'[35] Given the essay topic 'My Favourite Hero' at school, Joyce chose Ulysses.

In 1894 the family moved again to 13 North Richmond Street, formerly owned by a priest who had died in the back drawing room. Joyce describes the *musty* odour that *hung in all the rooms* in 'Araby', as well as the wild garden where he found the priest's *rusty bicycle-pump*.[36] The favoured son, he had the luxury of a room of his own. At school he was soon noted for his skill at English composition; he won essay competitions in 1894, 1895 and 1897 and used the money to buy presents and books and some pink paint for his bedroom, but the cash and the paint soon ran out.

Odysseus (the Roman's called him Ulysses) is the husband of Penelope and son and heir of Laertes, king of Ithaca. During the Trojan War he distinguished himself for bravery, cunning and eloquence. The *Odyssey* describes his long, wandering journey home to Ithaca (after encounters with the Cyclops, the Sirens, the enchantress Circe and the goddess Calypso, with whom he lived for eight years) and his eventual recognition as king.

One day in June 1895 the 13-year-old Joyce and his brother Stanislaus played truant from Belvedere. After crossing the River Liffey to Ringsend, they rested on the banks of the River Dodder, where they were approached by a paedophile, as Joyce later recalled in 'An Encounter' (1905). The strange man in this short story represents an adult world of dark desire that the boys can only dimly comprehend, but Joyce's own dawning sexual awareness is well illustrated by an episode that occurred in 1896. He was walking through fields at the edge of a wood with the family nanny when she suddenly excused herself and asked him to look away. Joyce 'jiggled furiously', aroused by the sound of her urinating.[37] It was a sound he was to evoke many times, as when

Leopold Bloom in *Ulysses* recalls his wife seated on the chamber pot: *Chamber music. Could make a kind of pun on that. It is a kind of music.*[38] His first poetry collection was called *Chamber Music* and he punningly referred to himself as a *chamber poet*.[39] Later, the hero of *Finnegans Wake* would be accused of spying on micturating girls. The event with the nanny was followed by a flirtation with a young maidservant, described by Stanislaus as 'a kind of catch-as-catch-can cum spanking match'.[40]

Joyce at 14 was sexually precocious and his restless desires sent him out into the city at night: *He wandered up and down the dark slimy streets peering into the gloom of lanes and doorways, listening eagerly for any sound. He moaned to himself like some baffled prowling beast. He wanted to sin with another of his kind, to force another being to sin with him and to exult with her in sin.*[41] Eventually, as he was walking home by the canal after an evening at the theatre, a prostitute took his arm and his virginity.

So began his occasional after-school visits to the brothel area known as 'Monto' (because it was near Montgomery Street), which he would call *nighttown* in *Ulysses*.[42] In this maze of narrow, dirty streets in the run-down north inner city, only Joyce could have experienced something like an epiphany. On the other hand, his meeting with the prostitute began a Jekyll-and-Hyde period of soul-searching in which he experienced a brief revival of religious devotion, praying and saying his rosary, as recounted at length in Chapter III of *A Portrait*. It was not to last. It was in fact the last gasp of his Catholicism.

At Belvedere Joyce served two terms as prefect of the Sodality of the Blessed Virgin Mary, but the extent of his own religious feeling was limited. It was not so much Catholicism that claimed his interest as a system of metaphors that he could adopt and adapt in his writing. He rebelled against the Church, but he could still enjoy the drama of its rituals. It was pure theatre. Perhaps this is why, in *Finnegans Wake*, God becomes Michael Gunn, the

The Athenian inventor Daedalus (meaning 'cunning artificer') lived in Crete under King Minos and Queen Pasiphaë. Angry with Minos, Poseidon (the God of the Sea) punished him by making Pasiphaë fall in love with a bull. Daedalus built her a wooden cow so that she could copulate with the animal and she gave birth to the Minotaur: half-man, half-bull.[43] Daedalus then constructed a labyrinth in which to keep the monster. When Daedalus advised Ariadne to give Theseus a ball of thread to help him escape from the labyrinth, Minos imprisoned Daedalus and his son Icarus in the labyrinth. They escaped on wings made from wax and feathers, but Icarus's wings melted when he flew too near to the sun and he drowned in the Aegean Sea.

Daedalus and Icarus (1869) by Lord Leighton

impresario of the Gaiety Theatre on King Street, Dublin (*that king's treat house*).[44] *Mr Makeall Gone* – God the creator and the destroyer – is in charge of the whole show.[45] Joyce was a superstitious man, however, and he regarded God as *a malevolent reality* on a level with natural dangers such as *dogs, horses, firearms, the sea, thunderstorms, machinery* and *the country roads at night.*[46]

At 16 he briefly considered the priesthood, but art would be his true calling. The crucial moment comes in Chapter IV of *A Portrait* when Stephen has a vision of his namesake, Daedalus, *the fabulous artificer . . . a hawklike man flying sunward over the sea.*[47] It is *the call of life to his soul*, not *the inhuman voice that had called him to the pale service of the altar*, but life itself in all its human, mortal, sexual innocence, cleansed of all life-denying dogma.[48] Suffused with a sense of liberated potential, Stephen commits himself wholeheartedly to the life of an artist.

The following vision of a girl standing in the waters off Sandymount Strand (a beach on Dublin Bay), hitching up her skirts to reveal her thighs and shamelessly enjoying *the worship of his eyes*, is the final clincher.[49] Stephen is filled with a sense of *profane joy* at her *mortal beauty*; mortal but sublime, because it is divine to affirm life in all its paradoxical *error and glory*, to accept one's place within the cycle of living things: *To live, to err, to fall, to triumph, to recreate life out of life!*[50]

During the latter part of the nineteenth century, 'realism' was a definite trend in European literature. The 'realists' insisted upon sincerity, accurate documentation and sociological insight and their subjects were taken from everyday life, usually from the working classes. Stendhal (1783–1842) and Balzac (1799–1850) are seen as precursors of 'realism'. Flaubert was claimed by the 'realists' because of the objectivity of his method and the authenticity of detail in his fiction, in particular *Madame Bovary* (1857).

However much he enjoyed reading Alexandre Dumas's *The Count of Monte Cristo* (1844) or tales of the Wild West as a child, Joyce did not become a writer of fantasy. His aesthetic, which developed gradually from his extensive reading, was a realist one, for the French novelist Gustave Flaubert (1821–80) was just one of the *subversive writers* he turned to after school.[51] Not for him the far-fetched imaginings to which he was temperamentally unsuited. Silent and watchful, the daily round of his existence was all the material he needed to become a writer. As Stephen says: *See this. Remember.*[52]

While Stanislaus kept a diary (for which Joyce scholars are grateful), his brother *scrabbled and scratched and scriobbled and skrevened nameless shamelessness about everybody ever he met.*[53] Nobody was safe. He paid special attention to his family and friends, carefully observing their characters and habits, and he collected stories, sometimes appropriating them as if they had happened to him. Once, when a friend asked Joyce if he had gathered material for a scene in *Ulysses* on a walk with him on Sandymount Strand, Joyce fell silent for a moment before admitting 'that during his school-days he had experimented in storywriting about happenings with persons of interest to him, and brought a few of these to George Dempsey [his English teacher – Mr Tate in *A Portrait*] for his comments.'[54]

These literary experiments left Joyce with the uncanny feeling that he had stepped outside *the limits of reality* or *had wandered out of existence*.[55] He was turning his

Henrik Ibsen (1828–1906) is regarded as the founder of modern drama. His career shows a gradual move towards small-town social dramas detailing the lives of ordinary people, then a reaction towards overtly symbolic theatre. His plays include *A Doll's House* (1879), *Ghosts* (1881), *An Enemy of the People* (1882), *Hedda Gabler* (1890), *The Master Builder* (1892) and *When We Dead Awaken* (1899).

life into words, which required a level of critical distance that suited his nature. He walked the streets of Dublin, notebook at the ready, and *chronicled with patience what he saw, detaching himself from it and testing its mortifying flavour in secret*.[56] The Jesuit missionary Matteo Ricci (1552–1610) trained his mind to create memory palaces into which he would place concepts, people and objects. Joyce was also interested in mnemonics (the art of improving the memory) and Dublin was his memory palace. He created a virtual Dublin, *a skeleton map of the city in his mind*.[57]

Joyce was a rather cocky senior boy at Belvedere and would arrive late for lessons and answer back in class. He read widely and near the end of his school years he encountered the work of the Norwegian dramatist Henrik Ibsen. Ibsen's controversial plays (*Ghosts*, for instance, is about venereal disease) could not be performed in Dublin and it was indecent even to mention his name in polite society, but Joyce responded to the playwright's artistic honesty. Ibsen was a realist, but like Joyce he also revelled in the symbolic dimensions of his art, a level of carefully crafted artifice. In his mid-thirties Ibsen had left Norway to live abroad, an idea that appealed to the young Joyce, who so identified with this key figure in modern literature that Ibsen's example sustained him throughout what might be called his Stephen Dedalus years.

The Dante of Dublin

When he applied for admission to University College in September 1898, Joyce described his father's occupation as *going in for competitions*, in recognition of the amount of time the unemployed John Joyce spent writing to magazines in the hope of a cash prize.[58] Disappointment and drink inflamed his father's fierce temper. He scolded his children at every opportunity and once, under the influence of drink, he tried to strangle May. James and Stanislaus intervened, jumping on their father's back to stop him.

In many respects Joyce had formed himself at Belvedere and by the time he entered university he had gone some way towards forging his own aesthetic philosophy. He would continue to meditate long and hard on the function of the artist in the modern world, borrowing ideas of truth and beauty from the Greek philosopher Aristotle (384–322 BC) and the Italian scholar St Thomas Aquinas (*c*.1225–74), as well as Flaubert and his favourite poets Lord Byron (1788–1824), Charles Baudelaire (1821–67), Stéphane Mallarmé (1842–98) and W B Yeats (1865–1939). He also admired *the cloistral silverveined prose* of John Henry Newman (1801–90).[59] Eventually, he would make the following famous pronouncement: *The artist, like the God of the creation, remains within or behind or beyond or above his*

University College Dublin was founded in 1908 by Royal Charter as a constituent college of the National University of Ireland. It was a lineal successor of an earlier University College Dublin founded in 1854 by Cardinal John Henry Newman, known as the Catholic University. In 1908 it became part of the National University of Ireland. Recent alumni include Bertie Ahern, John Bruton, Albert Reynolds, Dr Garret FitzGerald and Charles Haughey, all of whom became Taoiseach or Prime Minister of the Irish Republic.

Characters: Clancy, Byrne, Joyce

handiwork, invisible, refined out of existence, indifferent, paring his fingernails.[60] The act of creation is a vanishing act: the artist disappears leaving in his wake a perfectly self-contained work of art.

As a student Joyce affected an air of boredom. He was supercilious, cheeky, arrogant, pretentious and often slapdash in his work, but his acute intelligence intimidated his tutors and his peers. His nearsighted stare gave an impression of withering indifference. He was a typical student in many respects – he had a loud laugh (described as a whoop), creased clothes and disliked washing – but the variety and breadth of his reading set him apart. He spent many hours at the National Library of Ireland in Kildare Street discussing his aesthetic manifesto with the chief librarian, Thomas William Lyster, and his assistant William Kirkpatrick Magee. Later, Joyce would set an entire episode of *Ulysses* ('Scylla and Charybdis') in the National Library, where Stephen, Lyster and Magee ('John Eglinton') debate the relevance of Shakespeare's life to his work.

Joyce selected his friends carefully at university. His closest confidant was John Francis Byrne, who exerted a strong influence over Joyce and was his intellectual equal. Joyce sought him out for leisurely walks around Dublin, during which he would pick his brains. According to another friend, William Fallon, the student Joyce had begun 'to outline a lay-out for his works of art and the Dublinised types he should select. To that end, who better than "Jeffbyrne" who knew the Metropolis and its purlieus and shebeens through-and-through and where Joyce could make personal contact with his human material? Byrne was his trustworthy keeper.'[61]

The Gaelic League (*Connradh na Gaeilge*) was an organization for the revival of the Irish language. It was founded in 1893 with the Irish author and scholar Douglas Hyde (Dubhghlas de hIde) as its president.

Next there was a medical student, Vincent Cosgrave, who was less high-minded than Byrne and therefore willing to go with Joyce to Monto. Cosgrave regarded Joyce as the most remarkable man he had ever met, but their friendship was not to last.

George Clancy was the only one of his friends to call him 'James' rather than 'Joyce'. An ardent nationalist, he helped form a branch of the Gaelic League at university and persuaded Joyce to take lessons in Irish. Joyce attended classes for a while, but gave them up because the instructor Patrick Pearse (later a key figure in the Easter Rising of 1916) denigrated English. Joyce's love of the English language (*the most wonderful language in the world*) set him apart from his nationalist friends.[62] *If the Irish programme did not insist on the Irish language*, he observed much later, *I suppose I*

Joyce used his friends as models for characters in *A Portrait* and *Ulysses* (except Kettle, who appears in *Finnegans Wake* under his own name). Byrne is the model for 'Cranly'; Cosgrave for 'Lynch'; Clancy for 'Madden' and 'Davin'; Skeffington for 'McCann'; and Curran for 'Donovan'.

could call myself a nationalist. As it is, I am content to recognize myself an exile.[63]

Other student friends included Francis Sheehy Skeffington, a liberal pacifist, feminist and vegetarian; Constantine P Curran; and Thomas Kettle. All were to be seen lounging around the entrance to the National Library, arguing with each other and watching the world (and the girls) go by.

As part of his matriculation Joyce wrote an essay on subjugation that reveals his hatred of violence. Written in a self-consciously 'high' style full of biblical cadences it is an impressive performance for a 16 year old. Subjugation by force, he argues, will only result in *ill-will and rebellion*.[64] In the arts, on the other hand, a level of subjugation is necessary. The artist imposes order on the world and overcomes chaos (prefiguring T S Eliot's contention that 'there is no freedom in art').[65] In another matriculation essay, 'The Study of Languages', Joyce argues that literature is as intellectual as mathematics and deserves to be regarded as a science. Shakespeare (1564–1616) and Milton (1608–74) deal with facts and ideas as precisely as any scientist, he says, but literature can also remoralize humanity, whereas science can demoralize and lead to inhumanity. In this he anticipated one of the main tenets of Modernism that 'a great literary masterwork is made for minds quite as serious as those engaged in the science of medicine'.[66]

In October 1899 Joyce submitted a paper entitled 'Drama and Life' to the university's Literary and Historical Society. He took this first public statement of his artistic principles extremely seriously, poring over it until he could pronounce its argument *flawless at all points*.[67] In it he distances himself from the fanciful excesses of the Irish Revival and outlines his own realist aesthetic: *Life we must accept as we see it before our eyes, men and women as we meet them in the real world, not as we apprehend them in the world of faery. The great human comedy in which each has share, gives limitless scope to*

In the first half of the twentieth century the term Modernism is particularly associated with the writings of Joyce, T S Eliot (1888–1965), Ezra Pound (1885–1972) and Virginia Woolf (1882–1941). Technically, Modernism was marked by experimentalism and rejected the established rules, traditions and conventions of the past.

the true artist, today as yesterday and as in years gone.[68] Modern life might appear unheroic compared with the ancient epics, but *out of the dreary sameness of existence, a measure of dramatic life may be drawn. Even the most commonplace, the deadest among the living, may play a part in a great drama.*[69]

Offering a sneak preview to Clancy, Joyce grandly announced *This is the first of my explosives*, implying it was the beginning of a long campaign.[70] He also read it to his mother while she did the ironing. May, a keen reader before she married, was concerned that her clever son was reading *dangerous authors*.[71] Joyce lent her some Ibsen plays, which she guardedly admired. His father also tried reading Ibsen, but was disappointed to find it was not as risqué as he had been led to believe by the Irish press.

Joyce's interest in foreign writers was unusual and the complex artistic manifesto he derived from his reading was regarded with suspicion: *No-one would listen to his theories: no-one was interested in art*, he complains in *Stephen Hero*. Stephen's fellow students *regarded art as a continental vice . . . for an artist with them was a man who painted pictures. It was a bad sign for a man to show interest in anything but his examinations or his prospective 'job'. It was all very well to be able to talk about it but really art was all 'rot': besides it was probably immoral; they knew (or, at least, they had heard) about studios. They didn't want that kind of thing in their country. Talk about beauty, talk about rhythms, talk about esthetic – they knew what all the fine talk covered.*[72]

The Irish Revival (or Celtic Twilight) marked a resurgence of Irish nationalism in the late nineteenth century and flourished until the 1920s. Rejecting the influence of English literature, Irish writers turned to their own heritage, as advocated by the Gaelic League. They were interested in Irish mysticism, folklore and local myth. The poetry is Symbolist and marked by an enervated melancholy, as in Yeats's *The Celtic Twilight* (1893).

It comes as no surprise, then, that the Society's President, Father Delany, forbade Joyce from reading his paper. 'Drama and

Life' represented the worst kind of *modern freethinking* and Delany was unimpressed by the fact that a student at the university had been reading writers *who openly profess their atheistic doctrines and fill the minds of their readers with all the garbage of modern society.*[73] Joyce was furious – *So after all his trouble, thinking out his essay and composing his periods, this old fogey was about to prohibit it!* – but he was not to be silenced so easily.[74]

Ibsen was the sticking point. Delany was convinced that Ibsen was in favour of *free living* and *unbridled licence.*[75] He was reluctant to have the university associated with such revolutionary theories and it is a testament to Joyce's considerable powers of persuasion that Delany finally backed down. Nevertheless, he sounded a warning shot: *I do not predict much success for your advocacy in this country*, he said. *Our people have their faith and they are happy. They are faithful to their Church and the Church is sufficient for them.*[76]

When Joyce read 'Drama and Life' to the Society on 20 January 1900 it was roundly attacked. The students complained that *the moral welfare of the Irish people was menaced by such theories. They wanted no foreign filth . . . the Irish people had their own glorious literature where they could always find fresh ideals to spur them on to new patriotic endeavours.* Joyce was *a renegade from the Nationalist ranks: he professed cosmopolitism* [sic], along with an *insidious theory that art can be separated from morality.*[77] Joyce (who relished the idea that people *feared him as an infidel*) calmly and ably defended himself point by point and was rewarded with a round of applause.[78] 'Joyce, that was magnificent,' said one student afterwards, 'but you're raving mad!'[79]

On that same day he received an offer from the editor of the *Fortnightly Review* to review Ibsen's new play *When We Dead Awaken.* 'IBSEN'S NEW DRAMA' BY JAMES A. JOYCE appeared on 1 April 1900. In it Joyce praises Ibsen as the most original dramatist of the age and defends him against his critics. He especially admires the way Ibsen, in this play, has compressed the life of his characters *into the comparatively short space of two days* (Joyce, of course, would eventually write a novel about a single day).[80] Joyce's review brought him a level of notoriety at university. It even prompted Ibsen himself to write to the 18-year-old reviewer via William Archer, his translator. Joyce took Ibsen's letter of thanks as an omen that he was destined for greater things and replied, through Archer, that *the words of Ibsen I shall keep in my heart all my life*.[81]

In that same year he wrote *My Brilliant Career*, a play heavily influenced by Ibsen, and sent it to Archer, who encouraged him to write more. He wrote a verse play entitled *Dream Stuff* and poems that reveal the influence of the lyrical Yeats, but little of this early work survives. In March 1901, having taught himself the rudiments of the language, Joyce sent a long letter to Ibsen in Dano-Norwegian. He praised the playwright's *absolute indifference to public canons of art* and his *inward heroism*. Ibsen's personal battles were an inspiration, he said, *not the obvious material battles but those that were fought and won behind your forehead*.[82] A similar battle was taking place behind Joyce's own forehead against the Catholic Church and British rule. In *Ulysses* Stephen taps his brow, saying *in here it is I must kill the priest and the king*.[83]

At university Joyce began to write a series of what he called 'epiphanies'. The idea came to him one evening when he overheard a conversation between a man and a woman in Eccles Street on the steps of *one of those brown brick houses which seem the very incarnation of Irish paralysis*:

The Young Lady – (drawling discreetly) . . . O, yes . . . I was . . . at the . . . cha . . . pel . . .

The Young Gentleman – (inaudibly) . . . I . . . (again inaudibly) . . . I . . .

The Young Lady – (softly) . . . O . . . but you're . . . ve . . . ry . . . wick . . . ed . . .[84]

It was the ineffable triviality of this conversation that seemed to Joyce worth preserving for posterity, as well as the air of sordid mystery surrounding the young man's inaudible proposition. *This triviality made him think of collecting many such moments together in a book of epiphanies. By an epiphany he meant a sudden spiritual manifestation, whether in the vulgarity of speech or of gesture or in a memorable phase of the mind itself. He believed that it was for the man of letters to record these epiphanies with extreme care, seeing that they themselves are the most delicate and evanescent of moments.*[85]

Forty of Joyce's 'epiphanies' survive out of at least 75 written before 1904 and many of them surface again, reworked, in his mature fiction. Yeats summed them up best as 'a beautiful though immature and eccentric harmony of little prose descriptions and meditations'.[86] The 'epiphanies' seem to be waiting to become poems, but Joyce was searching for a form less restrictive than poetry.

The Joyce family was constantly transplanted, principally to avoid landlords and debt-collectors. In May 1900 they moved to 8 Royal Terrace, near to a lunatic asylum for nuns (Joyce could hear them screeching *Jesus! O Jesus! Jesus!*) and a year later to 32 Glengariff Parade, near Fogarty's grocery.[87] Joyce's ability to coldly sum up his fellow Dubliners is nicely illustrated in the short story 'Grace': *Mr Fogarty was a modest grocer . . . He had opened a small shop on Glasnevin Road where, he flattered himself, his manners would ingratiate him with the housewives of the district. He bore himself with a certain grace, complimented little children and spoke with a neat enunciation. He was not without culture.*[88]

Joyce reserved his greatest contempt for what he called the 'rabblement' (the phrase appears first in one of his 'epiphanies'). It was a grave mistake, in his view, for an artist to listen to the mob. It was the mob, after all, that had brought down Parnell, that paragon of proud, defiant individualism. And it was the mob, too, that had booed and hissed Yeats's *The Countess Kathleen* (1892), the first play to be performed by the Irish Literary Theatre. Joyce had refused to sign a protest against the play in the *Freeman's Journal* and had supported the theatre at its foundation in 1899. But in his next essay, 'The Day of the Rabblement' (October 1901), he accused it of having reneged on its promise. Instead of being a showcase for European playwrights like Ibsen, it had retreated into a narrow nationalism and *surrendered to the popular will . . . the Irish Literary Theatre must now be considered the property of the rabblement.*[89]

Dublin-born poet W B Yeats (1865–1939) was a key player in the Irish Revival and founded the Irish Literary Theatre Company in 1899, later the Abbey Theatre Company. Plays on Irish themes by Yeats, Sean O'Casey (1880–1964), G B Shaw (1856–1950) and J M Synge (1871–1909) made Dublin's Abbey Theatre renowned, but it is as a poet that Yeats is justly revered. His poetry has exerted a considerable influence on generations of Irish (and non-Irish) poets. A senator of the Irish Free State (1922–8), he received the Nobel Prize for Literature in 1923.

Joyce was convinced that the bourgeois tastes of the Irish public were impeding Ireland's artistic development, dragging it back to a fake Celtic past while modern Europe advanced. What did the people know of Flaubert's *Madame Bovary*, he argued, or *Il Fuoco* (*The Flame*, 1900) by the Italian novelist and poet Gabriele D'Annunzio (1863–1938), which he considered to be the most important achievement in the novel since Flaubert. *Il Fuoco* was on the Vatican's Index of Prohibited Books, which is partly why 'The Day of the Rabblement' was rejected by *St Stephen's*, the university magazine.

Joyce took his grievance to the very top, the President, but when that failed he published his essay at his own expense alongside a piece by Skeffington (also rejected by *St Stephen's*) advocating equal status for women students. Joyce was emerging as a Dublin 'character', famous for his erudite article on Ibsen and latterly as a 'Scorner of Mediocrity and Scourge of the Rabblement'.[90]

In February 1902 Joyce presented another paper to the Literary and Historical Society on the Irish poet James Clarence Mangan (1803–49). Back home, his 14-year-old brother George was seriously ill with typhoid fever, but the prospect of a death in the family seems only to have strengthened Joyce's belief in literary immortality. Through literature, *that great memory which is greater and more generous than our memory, no life, no moment of exaltation is ever lost*, he announced.[91] Joyce spent a lot of time at George's bedside singing what he regarded as the best lyric ever written, Yeats's 'Who Goes with Fergus?': 'And no more turn aside and brood / Upon love's bitter mystery . . .'[92] Eventually a priest was sent for to hear George's confession. Joyce held his brother's hand while May prayed. John Joyce, *who was not quite sober walked about the room on tiptoe*, crying *in little fits* from time to time.[93] George died shortly after midnight on 9 March 1902.

Joyce was not especially close to George – he was, in fact, *almost a stranger to him* – but this made his passing all the more devastating.[94] George had *literally never dared to live* – for Joyce, the greatest crime of all.[95] *What's the matter with you*, he told Stanislaus, *is that you're afraid to live. You and people like you. This city is suffering from hemiplegia of the will. I'm not afraid to live.*[96] Joyce sought to make amends for George's wasted life by consigning him to the great memory of literature, writing his death into *Stephen Hero*, though disguising him as a younger sister, Isabel. It is also the subject of some of his 'epiphanies', in one of which he describes watching over his brother's corpse. He pities George, but adds: *I cannot pray for him as the others do.*[97]

The Wanderer

Joyce was about to leave University College and his thoughts turned to a career. His father wanted him to become a clerk at the Guinness brewery, but Joyce had grander plans. He was attracted to law and to journalism, but in the end medicine won out and he registered at the Royal University Medical School in April 1902. Nevertheless, when he graduated in June with a degree in Modern Languages, his first thought was to make his presence felt in the Irish literary world.

He approached George Russell, who found Joyce as 'proud as Lucifer', but introduced him to Yeats, who was similarly struck by Joyce's 'colossal self-conceit'.[98] A joke that circulated in Dublin afterwards had Joyce saying to Yeats: *We have met too late: you are too old to be influenced by me.*[100] Yeats was fairer in his assessment

The Irish dramatist and poet George William Russell (1867–1935) wrote under the pseudonym 'AE' and did much to help the young Joyce, hence Stephen's joke in *Ulysses*: *AEIOU.*[99] He was editor of the *Irish Homestead* (1906–23) and the *Irish Statesman* (1923–30).

of Joyce's abilities. 'You have a very delicate talent,' he said, 'but I cannot say whether for prose or verse.'[101]

Joyce began his medical course in October, attending lectures in biology, physics and chemistry. He struggled to pay his expenses, but whereas Byrne was offered teaching work, Joyce was turned away. He suspected a vendetta against him because of his reputation as a freethinker. This was also the view of John Joyce, who encouraged his son to escape from reactionary Dublin and seek out the freer atmosphere of Europe.

Joyce needed little persuasion. He contacted the Faculté de Médecine in Paris to request admission and planned to teach

Joyce the graduate

English to support himself. *I shall try myself against the powers of the world*, he wrote to Lady Gregory (1852–1932), another leading light in the Irish Revival, hoping that she might send him a little financial encouragement. *And though I seem to have been driven out of my country here as a misbeliever I have found no man yet with a faith like mine.* He was already casting himself in the role of a spurned genius. *I want to achieve myself – little or great as I may be – for I know that there is no heresy or no philosophy which is so abhorrent to my church as a human being, and accordingly I am going to Paris.*[102]

In *A Portrait* the touching domestic details of Stephen's symbolic flight to the Continent are swept away by his famous mission statement: *Mother is putting my new secondhand clothes in order. She prays now, she says, that I may learn in my own life and away from home and friends what the heart is and what it feels. Amen. So be it. Welcome, O life! I go to encounter for the millionth time the reality of experience and to forge in the smithy of my soul the uncreated conscience of my race.*[103]

There is an economic and there is a spiritual exile. There are those who left her [Ireland] to seek the bread by which men live and there are others, nay, her most favoured children, who left her to seek in other lands that food of the spirit by which a nation of human beings is sustained in life.[104]

James Joyce, *Exiles* (1918)

Yeats suggested Joyce might turn his hand to book reviews and invited him to London. Clutching a letter from the Lord Mayor (a friend of his father's) that vouched for his good character, Joyce left Dublin on the evening of 1 December 1902. Yeats treated him like a star, covering his expenses and introducing him to many useful literary contacts. By the time Joyce took a seat on the train to Newhaven, he had secured a promise from the poet and critic Arthur Symons (1865–1945) to help him publish his poems.

In Paris Joyce stayed at the Hôtel Corneille in the Latin Quarter. This medieval part of the city is dominated by the Sorbonne, the most prestigious European university in the Middle Ages, and as Joyce walked the narrow, crooked streets he was following in the footsteps of his heroes St Thomas Aquinas and Dante Alighieri (1265–1321). Because of its student population, the area is generally associated with artists, intellectuals and a bohemian way of life. Joyce had spent most of his funds getting there, but made some money writing book reviews. He obtained a provisional card of admission to the École de Médecine and would take his first exam in July.

In his letters home Joyce professed to be much amused by Paris life, but in reality he was desperately homesick. His French was insufficient for the École's highly technical lectures, it was bitterly cold and his health was poor. He tried his best to make a go of things. He gave private English lessons to a champagne dealer; visited a theatre and a brothel; and had his photo taken in an ill-fitting overcoat. In the end, however, responding to the none-too-subtle hints in Joyce's letters, his father remortgaged the house in order to bring Sunny Jim home for Christmas.

From Paris Joyce had sent a photo-postcard of himself to Byrne inscribed with the poem that begins *All day I hear the noise of waters*. To Cosgrave, in contrast, he sent a postcard in dog Latin describing his adventures with the city's prostitutes. Cosgrave showed it to Byrne, who was not impressed. When Joyce returned to Dublin he found he had lost a friend. Byrne disapproved of his debauchery and predicted he would end up an alcoholic. Joyce prized Byrne's friendship highly and felt betrayed by his sanctimoniousness. In *A Portrait*, Cranly's coolness influences Stephen's

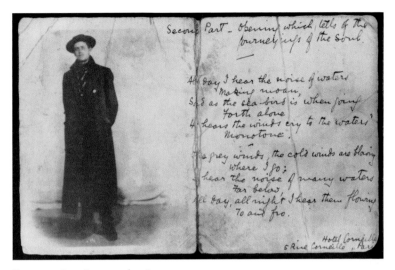

Second Part — Opening which tells of the
journeyings of the Soul.

All day I hear the noise of waters
Making moan;
Sad as the sea-bird is when going
Forth alone
He hears the winds cry to the waters'
Monotone.

The grey winds, the cold winds are blowing
Where I go;
I hear the noise of many waters
Far below,
All day all night I hear them flowing
To and fro.

Hotel Corneille
5 Rue Corneille, Par...

Paris poet: Joyce's postcard to Byrne

decision to leave Dublin: *Away then: it is time to go. A voice spoke softly to Stephen's lonely heart, bidding him go and telling him that his friendship was coming to an end.*[105]

Back in Paris on 23 January 1903, Joyce spent his days in the Bibliothèque Nationale on the Right Bank before moving on to the *studious silence* of the library of Saint-Geneviève on the Left Bank, where he *read, sheltered from the sin of Paris, night by night.*[106] He wrote aphorisms (signed and dated), poems (including *I hear an army charging upon the land* and *When the shy star goes forth in heaven*), some more epiphanies and a few book reviews. Isolated in Paris, he could develop as an artist far away from the pernicious influence of the Irish Revival. *And so help me devil I will write only the things that approve themselves to me and I will write them the best way I can.*[107]

By mid-February he was so poor he had to skimp on meals, although he still frequented the cafés, where he discussed litera-ture with other expatriates. He met the Irish playwright J M Synge, who left this impression of Joyce in a letter: 'He seems to be pretty badly off, and is wandering around Paris rather unbrushed and rather indolent, spending his studious moments in the National Library reading Ben Jonson. French literature I understand is beneath him!'[108]

Joyce also befriended another Irishman, Joseph Casey, who had a taste for absinthe and probably introduced him to *the green fairy*.[109] Joyce was a willing convert to this most 'ninetyish drink. He and Casey regularly lunched at a little restaurant on the rue du Louvre where they toasted each other's good health in Gaelic and talked *of lost leaders, the betrayed, wild escapes* – for Casey, a Fenian, had made a dramatic escape from Clerkenwell prison.[110] In *Ulysses* he is Kevin Egan, remembered with affection by Stephen as he wanders in the morning along the mudflats of Sandymount Strand.

Joyce was writing with greater self-confidence, but he was still searching for a style that would allow him complete freedom. Trawling through the Paris bookshops, he came upon a novel that struck him as revolutionary. Édouard Dujardin's *Les Lauriers sont coupés* tells the story of Daniel Prince, an ordinary Parisian, in whose wandering, irresolute mind the reader remains without interruption from 6 p.m. until midnight one April evening. Nothing much happens, though Daniel thinks a lot about Léa, a woman he has been chastely courting for far too long. Dujardin's experiment with psychological time uses accumulated images and recurrent thoughts and themes, attaining the subtlety of music. He called this technique *monologue intérieur* ('interior

The French novelist and Symbolist poet Édouard Dujardin (1861–1949) was a friend of Mallarmé and an admirer of the German composer Richard Wagner (1813–83). In 1885 he founded *la Revue wagnérienne*, an important Symbolist journal, but he is best remembered for his novel *Les Lauriers sont coupés* (1888, translated into English as *We'll to the Woods No More*, 1957). Joyce's acknowledged debt to this book made Dujardin famous in the last years of his life.

monologue'), though it is better known as 'stream of consciousness'. Many twentieth-century writers experimented with it, from Marcel Proust (1871–1922) and Dorothy Richardson (1873–1957) to Virginia Woolf (1882–1941) and William Faulkner (1897–1962), but Joyce was to make it his own in *Ulysses*.

The term 'stream of consciousness' was coined by the psychologist William James (1842–1910) in *Principles of Psychology* (1890) to denote the flow of inner experiences. In literary criticism it refers to any technique that seeks to depict the unspoken thoughts and emotions of a character without recourse to objective description. Dujardin was a pioneer of the technique, which marked a revolution in the modern novel.

Joyce believed he had a charmed life. From an early age, he was convinced he was a genius, if not a national treasure. *I should be supported at the expense of the state*, he once announced, and he threw himself on the charity of his friends and acquaintances without compunction.[111] He even offered to make himself a joint-stock company so he could sell shares to interested parties – they would provide for the struggling artist now, then profit from his literary success later. Despite some teaching work and the support of his Paris friends, however, he was kept awake at night with hunger pangs. His parents frequently visited the pawnshop in order to send him a little more money, but they were far from wealthy and his mother's health was deteriorating.

On 10 April 1903, Joyce returned late to his hotel to find a blue telegram waiting for him that immediately broke the spell of Paris: *Nother [sic] dying come home father*.[112] He scarcely had enough money for his next meal, let alone a ticket to Dublin, but before dawn he had persuaded a sympathetic and well-off pupil to stump up the cost. He crossed from Dieppe to Newhaven on the 11th.

May Joyce had been suffering from cancer for some time, but it had only recently been diagnosed. When her eldest son came home she pleaded with him from her deathbed to make his Easter

Duties, to confess his sins, do penance and receive Holy Communion. Joyce refused. It was the greatest trial of his beliefs that he would ever undergo and it scarred him deeply. In *Ulysses* Stephen recalls the white china bowl by his mother's bedside *holding the green sluggish bile which she had torn up from her rotting liver by fits of loud groaning vomiting.*[113]

Joyce discussed his dilemma with Byrne, as recorded in *A Portrait* where Stephen tells Cranly he has quarrelled with his mother about his Easter Duty. *Do as she wishes you to do*, advises Cranly. *What is it for you? You disbelieve in it. It is a form: nothing else. And you will set her mind at rest . . . Whatever else is unsure in this stinking dunghill of a world a mother's love is not.*[114]

May Joyce died on 13 August 1903, aged 44. Neither James nor Stanislaus could be persuaded to kneel at her bedside in her last hours. At midnight on the day of her death, May's ghost appeared to her daughter Margaret ('Poppie'). Joyce used her account of this visitation in *Ulysses* when Stephen sees his dead mother wearing *loose brown graveclothes*, her breath giving off *a faint odour of wetted ashes.*[114] Her second appearance sends him screaming from a brothel.

It was all change in the Joyce family after May's death. Poppie, who wanted to become a nun, had to take charge of the house instead (she became a Sister of Mercy six years later). For his part, Joyce took to brooding, Hamlet-like, on the state of the world, just as Stephen does in *Ulysses*. There is no doubt he felt guilty, but also angry: *My mother was slowly killed, I think, by my father's ill-treatment, by years of trouble, and by my cynical frankness of conduct. When I looked on her face as she lay in the coffin – a face grey and wasted with cancer – I understood that I was looking on the face of a victim and I cursed the system which had made her a victim.*[116]

Paris had changed Sunny Jim, though not necessarily for the better. He cut a bohemian figure in his broad-brimmed *Latin quarter hat* and wide Paris tie, swinging an ashplant (a type of cane) from side to side.[117] 'The gestures he made with the ashplant he now carried,' said a friend, 'his way of making his voice raucous, were surely part of an act. And wasn't there, too, in his behaviour, the assertion of a young man conscious of his hand-me-down clothes, whose resort was the pawn office, and who was familiar with the houses of Nighttown? The raucous voice, the obscene limericks delivered with such punctilio . . . Was he playing Rimbaud or Villon?'[118] Worse still, he wore a pointed beard that made him look like the devil.

Around this time Joyce met Oliver St John Gogarty, a medical student at Trinity College. Wealthy, talented, ambitious and witty (three of his bawdy songs appear in *Ulysses*), Gogarty went on to become a famous surgeon and poet. His nickname for the sharp-witted Joyce was *Kinch, the knifeblade*, but he also dubbed him the 'Dante of Dublin'.[119] Like Byrne, Gogarty was close to being Joyce's equal. He also agreed with Byrne that Joyce had wronged his mother. *You could have knelt down, damn it, Kinch, when your dying mother asked you*, says Mulligan (Gogarty) in *Ulysses, to think of your mother begging you with her last breath to kneel down and pray for her. And you refused. There is something sinister in you . . .*[120]

Joyce had also brought back from Paris a French cabaret song, 'Cadet Roussel', which he taught his friends to sing *in chorus, stamping their feet at every: – Ho! Ho! Hohé, vraiment!*[121] He became known as Cadet Roussel among his circle, but he was in danger of becoming another of Gogarty's comic creations, a Dublin 'character' like his father. Having taken a few steps down this path, he saw it for what it was: a dead-end. As one friend put it: 'Joyce recognised the futility of such a course. When he had gathered his swag he cleared out.'[122] The swag being 'his blotting-paper memory and a trunkful of notes'.[123] Joyce later said of Dublin, *I never really left it. I carry it around with me.*[124]

He had always been aloof, but now, having honed his superiority complex in sophisticated Paris, he could barely conceal his disdain at having to borrow money from people he considered beneath him in intellect and talent. This was not unjustified arrogance in Joyce's case, but it was a poor way to make friends and he paid for it dearly later.

He sought out the company of Gogarty, Cosgrave and another medical student, John Elwood ('Temple' in *A Portrait*) and they drank heavily in the pubs of Dublin. Joyce read a great deal, dabbling in socialism and anarchism and, like Mr Duffy the repressed bachelor in 'A Painful Case' (1905), he read Friedrich Nietzsche (1844–1900) at a time when the German philosopher was barely known in Europe, let alone Ireland. He wrote book reviews for the *Daily Express*, applied unsuccessfully for a job at the National Library, attended a few classes in law and medicine and even toyed with the idea of starting a daily newspaper to be called *The Goblin*, though nothing came of it. He was in a rut, but the new year would change all that.

Nora

Nora

The year 1904 set Joyce firmly on the road to being a great writer. On 7 January, in an exercise book belonging to his sister Mabel, he copied a short autobiographical essay-story entitled 'A Portrait of the Artist'.

The hero, Stephen Daedalus (later Dedalus), has the first name of a Christian martyr and the surname of an ancient Greek. It is a sympathetic self-portrait, though not uncritical: Joyce is aware of Stephen's egotism and immaturity, but he admires his dedication to art. For the next ten years James Joyce and Stephen would develop simultaneously (he even signed himself 'Stephen Daedalus' in letters to Gogarty). As Stephen, Joyce could depict himself as a sensitive artist surrounded by philistines and bourgeois hypocrites. In fact, he was not so alone as he liked to make out. Several of his contemporaries in the Irish literary movement were sympathetic towards European literature and admiring of Ibsen, but Joyce clung to his pose of cultivated isolation.

He sent 'A Portrait of the Artist' to Magee, the editor of a new journal, *Dana*. Magee rejected it as 'incomprehensible', but also too sexual, for it contained a highly charged vision of the girl Joyce had seen on Sandymount Strand in 1898. As Stanislaus recorded in his diary on 2 February 1904: 'Jim . . . has decided to turn his paper into a novel, and having come to that decision is glad, he says, that it was rejected . . . Jim is beginning his novel, as he usually begins things, half in anger, to show that in writing about himself he has a subject of more interest than their aimless discussion.'[125] Within a month Joyce had finished the first chapter of *Stephen Hero*.

Joyce was restless and unstable after his mother's death and

Giotto's St Stephen (1320–5)

St Stephen was the first Christian martyr. He was a Jew educated in Greek who 'did great wonders and miracles among the people', but was stoned to death for blasphemy: 'And they stoned Stephen . . . And he kneeled down, and cried with a loud voice, Lord, lay not this sin to their charge. And when he had said this, he fell asleep.' (Acts, 6:8; 7:60)

sought solace in drink. He briefly reconsidered a singing career and took part in a tenor competition at Dublin's annual Feis Ceoil (Festival of Music) in May. He sang two set pieces beautifully, but refused to perform a piece he had not prepared and walked off stage. The judge had intended to award him the gold medal, but Joyce had to settle for the bronze because he had broken the rules. Encouraged by his performance, Joyce left home and rented a room in Dublin to practise his singing, but he disliked discipline and soon gave up. He decided instead to be a school-teacher and taught for a few weeks at Clifton School in Dalkey (as later recalled in the 'Nestor' episode of *Ulysses*).

In June he fell in love. Previous love interests included his cousin Katsy Murray and an unrequited love for a neighbour, Mary Sheehy. Hitherto unlucky in love, he had learned all he knew of women in Monto, where he had recently caught a sexually transmitted disease. Joyce seems to have been incapable of wooing a girl from his own social sphere. *I never could speak to the girls I used to meet at houses*, he complained. *Their false manners checked me at once.*[126] He was shy with women and too self-conscious to be a gallant – he despised that kind of man anyway, as shown in his short story 'Two Gallants' (1906). But on 10 June he somehow plucked up the courage to speak to a girl with red-brown hair as she walked down Nassau Street. She was 20, from Galway in the west and a chambermaid and waitress-cum-barmaid at Finn's Hotel on Leinster Street. Her name was Nora Barnacle.

The 22-year-old Joyce cut a dashing figure in a yachting cap and canvas shoes and he persuaded this complete stranger to meet him again on 14 June at 8.30 p.m. beside Sir William Wilde's house at the corner of Merrion Square. He waited a long time, squinting at every redhead that passed, but Miss Barnacle did not appear. Either she had misgivings or could not get the evening off work. *I went home quite dejected*, he informed her in a note. *I would like to make an appointment but it might not suit you. I hope you will be kind enough to make one with me – if you have not forgotten me!*[127]

Nora had not forgotten. They met at the corner of Merrion Square on 16 June and walked eastwards past the docks and towards the deserted harbour at Ringsend. It was an odd place to go on a first date. As Joyce tells it, Nora *sauntered over to me and took me so easily into her arms and made me a man*.[128] Many years later, as a love token, the action of *Ulysses* would take place on 16 June 1904, the day Nora, quite literally, took him in hand.[129]

Four days later Joyce got blind drunk and caused a scene behind a grocer's in Camden Street at a rehearsal of the National Theatre Society. He collapsed in a passageway in his own *mulberrycoloured, multicoloured, multitudinous vomit*.[130] Another night around this time – emboldened perhaps by his success with Nora – he made advances to a young woman in St Stephen's Green, oblivious to the fact that she had a male companion. There was a fight, after which Joyce was left with *black eye, sprained wrist, sprained ankle, cut chin, cut hand*.[131] It was probably on this occasion that he was dusted off and taken home by a man named Alfred Hunter, who was rumoured to be Jewish and to have an unfaithful wife. Joyce

The artist as a young man (22)

was surprised that someone he barely knew and with whom he had nothing in common should come to his aid. It was another 'epiphany' and gave him an idea for a story.

Despite these drunken shenanigans, he continued to court Nora. They would meet in the evening and walk through the streets, then down by the canal. Joyce was totally candid from the start: Nora would have to accept him warts and all. *There is something also a little devilish in me*, he wrote to her, *that makes me delight in breaking down people's ideas of me and proving to them that I am really selfish, proud, cunning and regardless of others.*[132] He made no secret of his sexual exploits or of his renunciation of Ireland and its religion. *My mind rejects the whole present social order and Christianity – home, the recognised virtues, classes of life, and religious doctrines.* As for the Catholic Church, *I make open war upon it by what I write and say and do.*[133]

It was fighting talk, yet around this time he was also writing the gentle, lyrical poems that were to be collected in *Chamber Music* (1907), which he dedicated to Nora (*chambermade music* he calls it in *Finnegans Wake*).[134] Later, he tended to disparage these simple lyrics, though they proved an effective seduction tool as proof of his romantic sensitivity. They are formal exercises modelled on the Elizabethan lyricists and the airs of John Dowland (1563–1626). Written more to be sung than to be read, they have been dismissed as 'a product of the drawing-room sentimentalist in Joyce'.[135] He admitted to having *an oldfashioned ear* when it came to poetry, though, ironically, the inclusion of the poem *I hear an army charging upon the land* in Ezra Pound's influential anthology of Imagist verse brought Joyce into the charmed circle of the avant-garde.[136]

Words for music, perhaps

While hard at work on *Stephen Hero*, Joyce was asked by George Russell if he would write a short story for the *Irish Homestead*, the weekly journal of the Irish Agricultural Organization Society. In July 1904, with seemingly little effort, Joyce came up with 'The Sisters', for which he was paid a sovereign. Encouraged, he began planning a book of ten stories. *I call the series Dubliners*, he told Curran, *to betray the soul of that hemiplagia or paralysis which many consider a city.*[137]

'The Sisters' appeared in the *Homestead* on the first anniversary of his mother's death. (Ashamed of writing for *the pigs' paper*, Joyce used the pseudonym 'Stephen Daedalus'.)[138] Another story, 'Eveline', was published in

The American poet Ezra Pound (1885–1972) championed the work of Joyce, T S Eliot and Wyndham Lewis (1882–1957). During the Second World War Pound's anti-democratic, pro-fascist broadcasts from Italy led to his being arrested by the Allies in 1945 and interned at Pisa (where he wrote the *Pisan Cantos*). Confined to a mental institution until 1958, he died in Italy.

September and 'After the Race' in December, but the *Homestead* rejected his next story, 'Hallow Eve' ('Clay' in *Dubliners*) and asked him not to send any more – there had been too many letters of complaint.

Curran was editing *St Stephen's* and asked Joyce for a contribution. Seizing the opportunity to settle a few scores, he sent him a long satirical poem in rhyming couplets. In 'The Holy Office' Joyce stakes out his territory and dissociates himself from the Abbey Theatre and the Irish Revival. *But I must not accounted be / One of that mumming company*, he says, which included (without actually naming names) Lady Gregory, Yeats, Synge, Gogarty, Russell and others.[139] Joyce was no dreamy Celtic Twilight aesthete and later professed to be *nauseated by their lying drivel about pure men and pure women and spiritual love and love for ever: blatant lying in the face of the truth*.[140] He would hold up his mirror to the world, unsparing in his sincerity. Writing, for Joyce, was a holy office and his artistic programme could include the most profane and sordid reality: *But all these men of whom I speak / Make me the sewer of their clique. / That they may dream their dreamy dreams / I carry off their filthy streams*.[141] Joyce had no time for Celtic melancholy. Later he would ask: *What is wrong with all these Irish writers – what the blazes are they always snivelling about?* and would sum up contemporary Irish literature as *ill-written, morally obtuse formless caricature*.[142]

'The Holy Office' lost Joyce a lot of friends and potential allies, as anticipated in the defiant final couplet: *And though they spurn me from their door / My soul shall spurn them evermore*.[143] It was far too scabrous to appear in *St Stephen's*, but Joyce could not afford to have it printed privately without the financial aid of the people he had lambasted.

Meeting Nora gave him the confidence to make a clean break. In one of his poems he says to her:

Because your voice was at my side
  I gave him pain,
Because within my hand I held
  Your hand again.

There is no word nor any sign
  Can make amend –
He is a stranger to me now
  Who was my friend.[144]

The friend in question was Gogarty, who objected to being caricatured in 'The Holy Office' as a snob. *He fears the lancet of my art,* noted Joyce, *as I fear that of his.*[145] He was contemplating leaving Dublin again, though a more pressing concern was the need to vacate his rented rooms. He had no intention of returning home, so in September he ended up staying with Gogarty. It proved a major turning point in his life.

Gogarty was living in a Martello Tower (a small circular fort) on Dublin Bay, which he rented from the Secretary of State for War. Originally built to defend the Irish coast against invasion by Napoleon, the tower was 40 feet high with eight-foot-thick walls and could be entered only by a ladder. Gogarty shared it with Samuel Chenevix Trench, an Anglo-Irishman so enamoured of the Irish Revival that he had changed his name to Dermot. Trench was a disturbed character (he shot himself in 1909) and Joyce had good reason to be wary of him.

This was confirmed on the night of 15 September 1904. Trench awoke screaming from a nightmare in which a black panther was attacking him. He reached for his revolver and shot at the fireplace near to where Joyce was sleeping. Afterwards Trench fell asleep, but soon woke again raving about a panther. Not to be outdone, Gogarty grabbed his own gun, saying 'Leave him to me!'

The Martello Tower, Bloomsday 1964

and shot at the pots and pans directly above Joyce's head. Joyce was too angry or scared to say anything. He dressed quickly, climbed down the ladder and marched off into the night.

Stanislaus records in his diary that Gogarty had wanted Joyce to leave, but was worried that if Joyce did 'make a name some day' it would look bad. 'Jim is determined,' noted Stanislaus, 'that if Gogarty puts him out it will be done publicly.'[146] As Cosgrave told Stanislaus, with *Stephen Hero* in mind: 'I wouldn't like to be Gogarty when your brother comes to the Tower episode. Thanks be to God I never kicked his arse or anything.'[147] But *Stephen Hero* never got that far: the 'Tower episode' was reserved for the opening of *Ulysses*, when Stephen complains to Mulligan (Gogarty) that Haines (Trench) has been *raving all night about a black panther* and wonders where he keeps his gun. He is frightened, *Out here in the dark with a man I don't know raving and moaning to himself about shooting a black panther . . . I'm not a hero . . . If he stays on here I am off.*[148]

Stephen is spared the indignity of being shot at. He simply leaves for work, resolved never to return to the tower. In reality a shaken Joyce walked all the way from Sandymount to Fairview, where he stayed for a few days with his aunt and uncle, Josephine and William Murray ('Richie Goulding' in *Ulysses*), before returning to the family home.

Two days later he poured out his hatred of Dublin to Nora. *When I was waiting for you last night I was even more restless. It seemed to me that I was fighting a battle with every religious and social force in Ireland for you and that I had nothing to rely on but myself. There is no life here – no naturalness or honesty. People live together in the same houses all their lives and at the end they are as far apart as ever.*[149] He had already asked her to run away with him the day before the tower incident. Nora, who cared little for her job and had a reckless streak, approved of the plan. Joyce admired her courage. *The fact that you can choose to stand beside me in this way in my hazardous life fills me with great pride and joy*, he wrote.[150] He asked Byrne's opinion about eloping with Nora. 'Don't wait,' said Byrne, 'and don't hesitate.'[151]

Joyce dreamt of a new life in Paris. It would be a grand gesture, an adventure, but also, as he told Nora, *it amuses me to think of the effect the news of it will cause in my circle. However, when we are once safely settled in the Latin quarter they can talk as much as they like.*[152] From Paris they would travel to Switzerland, where Joyce would teach English at a Berlitz School in Zurich. It sounded perfect.

Joyce and Nora scraped together enough money to get them to Paris. It was Nora, rather than Joyce, who took the greatest risk.

In those days a woman's reputation meant everything and she was running away, unmarried, without informing her family. She had no French and no means of supporting herself abroad if the curious young man she had fallen in love with chose to abandon her. But Nora had the courage to make a leap of faith into the unknown, unlike Eveline, in Joyce's short story of that name. At the last minute, with her lover already aboard the ship heading for Argentina, Eveline draws back from the new life that is offered her and clings to the security of Dublin *like a helpless animal*.[153] Nora would not make the same mistake.

Maximilian Berlitz (1852–1921) gave his name to the first Berlitz School of Languages founded in 1878 in Rhode Island, USA, and the Berlitz method of language instruction. There are now hundreds of Berlitz schools all over the world.

Self exiled in upon his ego[154]

Joyce and Nora arrived in London in October 1904 and he left her in a public park while he sought out Symons to get an advance for *Chamber Music*. It must have been a tense few hours for Nora, wondering if he would ever return. He did, but without any money, for Symons had been out. That night they travelled to Paris and the following day Nora was again left waiting in a park while Joyce borrowed money from various friends and acquaintances. Two days later they were in Switzerland, staying at the Gasthaus Hoffnung in Zurich.

On the morning of their arrival Joyce visited the Berlitz School only to make the alarming discovery that there was no job waiting for him. Fortunately there was a position free in Trieste, then a part of the Austro-Hungarian Empire. Weary of travelling, they arrived in Trieste on 20 October and an hour or so later Joyce was in jail, having rashly intervened on behalf of three drunken English sailors who were arguing with the police. After some wrangling, the British consul had Joyce released, but his run of bad luck continued: there was no job in Trieste either.

Joyce secretly relished being thrown back on his resources and at this stage in his life his gift of the gab proved far more useful than any literary talent. He borrowed money left, right and centre from everyone he could. At the same time he wrote another chapter of *Stephen Hero* and a short story ('Clay') about his Uncle William. Eventually, almost miraculously, a teaching post became available at a Berlitz School south of Trieste in Pola (now Pulj in Croatia), down the Adriatic coast at the tip of the Istrian peninsula. Nora and Joyce were on the move again.

Joyce spoke the old-fashioned Italian of a scholar, so one of the first things he did in Pola was take lessons in Tuscan Italian. A talented linguist, he quickly mastered its dialect and accents. Joyce was a survivor with a charmed life and an unshakeable sense of his own worth, but Nora had been dragged away from her life in Ireland to an unfamiliar land where she did not speak the language. She could not settle and was terribly homesick. It was winter and they lived in a tiny room without a stove.

Joyce continued to work on *Stephen Hero*, sitting on the bed and peering at his notes through pince-nez. Being a *voluntary exile* sounded grand, but it had its drawbacks.[155] He missed being able to bounce ideas off his few remaining friends in Dublin, though he sent some chapters to Stanislaus, whose praise bolstered his confidence.

Berlitz School (centre) at Trieste

Joyce disliked teaching, but with the little money he made he had his teeth fixed and bought a pork-pie hat and a much-needed new suit. He grew a moustache and cultivated the air of a dandy. He and Nora settled into a comforting domestic routine, albeit on a shoestring and not without its quarrels. They were still getting to know one another and Joyce often quizzed her about her past. *She has had many love-affairs*, he confided to Stanislaus, *one when quite young with a boy who died.*[156] The effect of this revelation on Joyce can perhaps be gauged by his use of it in 'The Dead' (1907).

Joyce wanted someone to buy *Chamber Music*, for he desperately needed the money. Nora was pregnant and Joyce asked Stanislaus to send him any information he could about embryology. The subject had fascinated him ever since he had spotted the word *Fœtus* scratched on a desk in Queen's College, Cork, in 1894.[157] The expectant parents were at least offered a better flat with a stove and a writing desk. They moved in January 1905, but in March, without warning, the Austrian authorities decided to expel all foreigners from Pola to break up a spy ring. Joyce was immediately transferred to Trieste, dragging a miserable Nora with him.

He felt more at home in Trieste, relishing its cosmopolitan mix of nationalities – Greeks, Austrians, Hungarians and Italians. The landlady of their first flat did not want a baby in the building, but fortunately they found a better room in a house next door to the Berlitz School where Joyce began to teach. He was constantly in debt, however, so it came as a blow in May when the publisher Grant Richards turned down *Chamber Music*.

He began to feel the weight of his responsibilities. Had he escaped the paralysis of Dublin only to set a trap of his own making? Nora was equally unhappy and Joyce confessed to his brother: *I do not know what strange morose creature she will bring forth after all her tears.*[158] His domestic difficulties also poisoned his attitude to his homeland. He felt that Ireland had expelled him, if not physically then spiritually. Still bitter at the way Gogarty and others had treated him, he scraped together enough money to have 'The Holy Office' printed. He sent it to Stanislaus, who distributed it in Dublin. Whether Joyce's grievances were real or imagined (being shot at was real enough), writing was the surest means of revenge: *Give me for Christ' sake a pen and an ink-bottle and some peace of mind and then, by the crucified Jaysus, if I don't sharpen that little pen and dip it into fermented ink and write tiny little sentences about the people who betrayed me send me to hell.*[159]

On 27 July 1905 Stanislaus received a laconic telegram: *Son born Jim.*[160] Joyce named the child Giorgio, after his dead brother George. He was adamant the baby would not be baptized, but Nora, who had not abandoned her faith, secretly saw to the matter in Dublin in 1912. Becoming a father is an important milestone and the 23-year-old Joyce felt changed by the experience: *The most important thing that can happen to a man is the birth of a child.*[161]

The short stories kept on coming: 'A Painful Case' by May; 'The Boarding House' and 'Counterparts' by July; 'Ivy Day in the Committee Room', 'An Encounter' and 'A Mother' by September; and 'Grace' by October. They came so quickly Joyce wondered if he was wasting his talent. *I am not rewarded by any feeling of having overcome difficulties*, he complained to Stanislaus. *Is it possible that, after all, men of letters are no more than entertainers?*[162] That thought was anathema to the author of 'The Holy Office'. He was an artist not an entertainer and he would seek out more and more difficulties to overcome, until, in the end, he would write the greatest experimental novel of all time, *Finnegans Wake*.

In the autumn Stanislaus finally caved in to Joyce's constant requests for him to come to Trieste. Arriving in October, he took a room next to his brother's and also began teaching at the Berlitz School. Touched by Joyce's straitened circumstances, he set a dangerous precedent by offering up his salary to pay household expenses. Soon he was regularly handing over more than he could afford.

Joyce refused to curb his extravagant lifestyle, much to Nora's chagrin. *I daresay I am a difficult person for any woman to put up with*, he admitted, *but on the other hand I have no intention of changing.*[163] He insisted on dining out every night, while Stanislaus ate a boiled egg at home. Then Stanislaus would set off (at Nora's request) to track down his brother in some late-night café and drag him away, Joyce singing a Triestine drinking song at the top of his voice.

Alcohol offered a blessed relief from his responsibilities. He felt trapped and was not leading the free and happy life of an artist. He briefly considered leaving Nora, but for all his failings Joyce was not the sort of man to walk out on the mother of his child. He respected parenthood and enjoyed being a father. And he loved Nora, whose loyalty impressed him, in stark contrast to the betrayal of his male friends. Women, it seemed, stood by him and this remained a constant throughout his life. The secret of Nora's success with Joyce was that she knew how to cut him down to size whenever he put on airs. She showed little interest in his books, but worse than her apparent indifference to his art was her tendency to lump him in with the other men she had known. This exasperated Joyce, who prided himself on being unique.

His brother's keeper: Stanislaus

In February 1906 he received a long-overdue boost to his confidence. Grant Richards agreed to publish the 12 stories of *Dubliners* that Joyce had sent him in December. Overjoyed, Joyce added another story, 'Two Gallants', and was inspired to write 'A Little Cloud', which he posted in April. But trouble was brewing. The Dublin printer objected to certain passages and changes would have to be made. Outraged that the printer had *descended with his blue pencil, full of the holy Ghost,* Joyce refused to alter a word. *It is not my fault that the odour of ashpits and old weeds and offal hangs round my stories,* he informed Richards. *I seriously believe that you will retard the course of civilization in Ireland by preventing the Irish people from having one good look at themselves in my nicely polished looking-glass.*[164]

Meanwhile the Berlitz School could not afford to pay Stanislaus and Joyce to teach English, so Joyce began to look for work elsewhere. In August he took Nora and Giorgio to Rome where he was on a two-month trial as a foreign correspondent in a bank. The job was dull and he was required to write hundreds of letters every day – worse still, he couldn't find a decent café and there were far too many tourists. Even with handouts from Stanislaus, Joyce was constantly short of funds (though he somehow wrangled a loan of 50 lire from the English consul in Rome). He began to offer private English lessons after work to supplement his income and taught at another language school, the École des Langues.

I have a new story for Dubliners in my head, he wrote to Stanislaus in September. *It deals with Mr Hunter* – the Jewish Dubliner who had come to his aid in St Stephen's Green in 1904.[165] The story was to be called 'Ulysses' (Joyce pronounced it 'Oolissays') and another title he had in mind for *Dubliners* was *Ulysses in Dublin*.

He felt a certain sympathy for – even a kinship with – Jews. Like him (in his more self-aggrandizing moments) they were ever-wandering perpetual exiles in a hostile world. And Ulysses had fascinated Joyce ever since he had discovered Charles Lamb's adaptation of the *Odyssey*. Lamb might also have given Joyce the idea of writing about a modern Ulysses, for as Lamb says of his *Adventures of Ulysses*: 'The ground-work of the story is as old as the *Odyssey*, but the moral and the colouring are comparatively modern.' Similarly, Lamb suggests that the giants, enchanters and sirens in Homer's epic are both real and also 'internal temptations' that one might encounter in everyday life. Much later, in his novel *Ulysses*, Joyce would make the sirens flirtatious barmaids, and the Cyclops, rather than a one-eyed giant, is a narrow-minded nationalist.

At the end of September Richards abruptly withdrew his offer to publish *Dubliners*, though he expressed interest in *Stephen Hero*. It was a major blow, but Joyce thought he could talk him round.

He agreed to remove 'Two Gallants' and 'A Little Cloud' and to modify the language in 'Counterparts' and 'Grace', but Richards had lost interest.

Arthur Symons's promise to help publish *Chamber Music* came good in October when another Dublin publisher, Elkin Mathews, finally accepted it for publication. But Joyce received the news without enthusiasm. The whole process had dragged on for too long and he dismissed his first published work as *a young man's book*, although some of the poems were *pretty enough to be put to music*.[166] He was never as sure of his poetry as he was of his prose. *A page of 'A Little Cloud' gives me more pleasure than all my verse*, he said.[167] Nora showed a rare interest in his first book of poems and he told her: *When I wrote them I was a strange lonely boy, walking about by myself at night and thinking that some day a girl would love me*.[168] Ezra Pound noted that the poems owed much to Joyce's 'strict musical training' and praised their 'clear-cut ivory finish'.[169] 'The inspiration of the book is almost entirely literary,' noted Joyce's old friend Kettle in the *Freeman's Journal*. 'There is no trace of the folklore, folk dialect, or even national feeling that have covered the work of practically every writer in contemporary Ireland.'[170] Joyce took this as a compliment and regarded Kettle as *the best friend I have in Ireland, I think*.[171]

In December Joyce and Nora moved to two rooms at 51 via Monte Brianzo. There was one *small-sized bed*, so they slept head to toe, like Bloom and his wife in *Ulysses*.[172] Meanwhile *the story about Hunter* would not come as easily as the other tales in *Dubliners*.[173] In February 1907 Joyce admitted to Stanislaus that 'Ulysses' had *never got any forrader than the title*.[174] He was having more luck with 'The Dead', the final story in *Dubliners* and generally regarded as his best.

He once described himself to Nora as a man *absurdly jealous of the past*, meaning her past, and this is precisely the predicament of Gabriel Conroy in 'The Dead'.[175] At the end of an evening of music and dancing, he watches his wife Gretta as she listens intently to the folk ballad 'The Lass of Aughrim'. Afterwards, at their hotel, Gabriel feels *a keen pang of lust* for her, but she seems distracted.[176] He is shocked when she tells him about Michael Furey, a delicate 17 year old who fell in love with her in Galway and used to serenade her with 'The Lass of Aughrim'. Furey stood in the rain at the end of her garden *and said he did not want to live* the night before Gretta left Galway for a Dublin convent. He died a week later. *I think he died for me*, she adds.[177]

How can Gabriel ever compete with Gretta's first love? Haunted by the image *of a young man standing under a dripping tree*, his thoughts turn towards his own mortality and the death of everyone.[178] The story ends with a famous vision – Gabriel's epiphany – of *the snow falling faintly through the universe and faintly falling, like the descent of their last end, upon all the living and the dead.*[179]

Nora had a real Michael Furey in her past – two, in fact. Michael Feeney was almost 17 when he fell in love with the 13-year-old Nora. He died of typhoid and was buried in Rahoon, a suburb of Galway City. Another admirer, Michael Bodkin, died at 20 and was also laid to rest at Rahoon. In 1912 Joyce would visit Rahoon Cemetery and brood upon Nora's sweethearts. The following year he wrote the poem 'She Weeps Over Rahoon', which begins *Rain on Rahoon falls softly, softly falling, / Where my dark lover lies.*[180] In his notes for the play *Exiles* he wrote: *She weeps over Rahoon, over him whom her love has killed, the dark boy whom, as the earth, she embraces in death and disintegration. He is her buried life, her past.*[181]

Isolated in Rome, Joyce worried about his *mental extinction.*[182] It was frustrating to be cut off from the literary and political debates in Ireland. He asked Aunt Josephine to send him newspapers, magazines and anything to do with his homeland. He was sick of Italy and his dislike of Rome made him reassess his attitude to

Dublin. Had he been wrong to concentrate only on Dublin's seamier side in *Dubliners?* Viewed from a nostalgic distance Dublin seemed to him the most hospitable city in Europe.

In February *Dubliners* was rejected by yet another publisher and Joyce decided to return with Nora (who was pregnant again) and Giorgio to Trieste. *My mouth is full of decayed teeth*, he told Stanislaus, *and my soul of decayed ambitions.*[183] To add injury to insult, shortly before he left Rome he was knocked down and his money stolen after a drinking binge.

Joyce and his family moved in with Stanislaus to save money, although Joyce continued to drink heavily despite Nora's protestations. He gave private lessons in English, but was also commissioned to write a series of articles on the 'Irish question' for the Italian newspaper *Il Piccolo della Sera.* Politically, Joyce was hardly a revolutionary. He was a Parnellite, like his father, and broadly sympathetic towards Fenianism, the subject of his first article in March 1907. The Fenians disbanded when their leader was arrested by the British. *Why this collapse of such a well-organized movement?* asked Joyce. *Simply because in Ireland, just at the crucial moment, an informer appears.*[184] After a rash of republican violence (including the Phoenix Park Murders), the forces of Fenianism regrouped in Sinn Féin and *this latest form of Fenianism*, observed Joyce, *may be the most formidable.*[185] He had always supported Ireland's right to govern itself and he welcomed Sinn Féin's policy of an economic boycott of Britain as *the highest form of political warfare.*[186] More articles followed: 'Home Rule Comes of Age' (May 1907), 'Ireland at the Bar' (September 1907), 'Oscar Wilde: The Poet of Salome' (March 1909), 'The Battle between Bernard Shaw and the Censor' (September 1909), 'The Home Rule Comet' (December 1910),

Fenians were members of a secret Irish-American revolutionary society, the Irish Republican Brotherhood (IRB), formed in 1858. The IRB was eventually replaced by Sinn Féin and the Irish Republican Army (IRA).

'The Shade of Parnell' (May 1912), 'The City of the Tribes' (August 1912) and 'The Mirage of the Fisherman of Aran' (September 1912).[187] Joyce was proud of these articles and even considered publishing them in English, though his low opinion of their literary value prevented him from pursuing the matter.

Il Piccolo gave Joyce the chance to air his political views in a more direct manner than he allowed himself to in his fiction. He was also invited to give three lectures on Ireland at the Università del Popolo in Trieste, in the first of which, 'Ireland, Island of Saints and Sages' (April 1907), he summed up the position of the Irish writer: *The economic and intellectual conditions of his homeland do not permit the individual to develop. The spirit of his homeland has been weakened by centuries of useless struggle and broken treaties. Individual initiative has been paralysed by the influence and admonitions of the church, while the body has been shackled by peelers, duty officers and soldiers. No self-respecting person wants to stay in Ireland.*[188]

Joyce's fierce individualism prevented him from joining any political party, but he was attracted to socialism as a state in which the individual and the artist might flourish – much as Oscar Wilde (1854–1900) predicts in *The Soul of Man Under Socialism* (1891). A life of grinding poverty made him favour the redistribution of wealth, but Joyce wanted nothing more from politicians than to be left alone to follow his own path in life with an absolute minimum of restraint. *As an artist*, he said, *I am against any State . . . the State is concentric, man is eccentric. Thence arises an eternal struggle.*[189] For a while he regarded himself as a pacifist anarchist like Shem in *Finnegans Wake*: *anarchistically respectsful of the liberties of the noninvasive individual.*[190] *Finnegans Wake* is perhaps his most political book, albeit a *politicoecomedy.*[191] Joyce's Finnegans are ordinary men and women throughout history and when they awaken it is simultaneously a resurrection and an insurrection.

In April 1907 John Joyce made it clear that he disapproved of his son's elopement with a socially inferior Galway woman. Joyce had made a 'miserable mistake' and ruined 'a life of promise' and a 'future that might have been brilliant'.[192] This intervention was unlikely to lift Joyce's spirits and to make matters worse he had grown dissatisfied with *Stephen Hero*. As with *Dubliners*, he felt anyone could have done it and wanted to try something new, to make *extravagant excursions into forbidden territory*.[193] He began to rewrite it, but even the rewrites struck him as too conventional. In May, sitting in a Triestine trattoria with Stanislaus, he suddenly pointed to a young man a little the worse for drink: *I would like to put on paper the thousand complexities in his mind*, he announced.[194] But how to do it?

In mid-July he was hospitalized with an attack of rheumatic fever, probably brought on by his nights lying in Italian streets, and then, on 26 July, Nora gave birth to a girl. They named her Lucia, after the patron saint of eyesight, although, ironically, it was around this time that Joyce's eye trouble began, exacerbated by his illness and his drinking.

By November Joyce had decided to turn his unfinished story 'Ulysses' into a novella, but in that same month the publisher of *Chamber Music* rejected *Dubliners*. Even for a writer with almost superhuman reserves of self-confidence this was a serious blow. He had dreamed of returning to Dublin as a success, but there was no virtue in being an

The virgin martyr Saint Lucia is the patron saint of Syracuse, Sicily, where she lived and died (in AD 304). She is the patron saint of sight and of the blind and was depicted by medieval artists carrying a dish containing her eyes.

Schmitz with his wife Livia and daughter Letizia

unpublished writer. It was hard to begin anything new with so many rejections and Joyce abandoned 'Ulysses' again in favour of his autobiographical novel, which he was to rework entirely under the title *A Portrait of the Artist as a Young Man*.

In this second attempt Joyce finally found the central idea that would govern his narrative. Like Dujardin before him, he began to experiment with the way a character's mental state might affect the prose style. The language of *A Portrait* reflects Stephen's mental development, moving from the childish naivety of the opening sections through to troubled schoolboy, romantic adolescent and, eventually, a young man scornful of his compatriots and bent on determining his own destiny. In short, it reveals the gradual gestation of Stephen's soul and in the last chapter, in which he records his thoughts in a diary, we see the beginnings of the stream of consciousness technique. This performative link between language and character was an important discovery for Joyce. The conventional, omniscient narrator of *Dubliners* was no longer necessary. Instead, a character's mental state could infect the style of the narrative. Later, in *Ulysses*, if a character is tired, the narrative is tired ('Eumaeus'). If a character is drunk, the narrative gets drunk too (the end of 'Oxen of the Sun').

Joyce renounced alcohol in February 1908, but soon fell back into his old ways. In August Nora had a miscarriage and he carefully examined the foetus. He revered birth and was sorry for this third child's *truncated existence*.[195] By the summer he was full of plans: he would become a commission agent for Irish tweeds or a professional tenor or go for a teaching post in Florence, but much of the year was taken up with family troubles and continued poverty. One of his pupils, Ettore Schmitz, confessed to having published two neglected novels, *Una Vita* (1892) and *Senilità* (1898), under the pseudonym Italo Svevo. Joyce read them and encouraged him to keep writing. Schmitz was a useful source of information about Judaism and his reciprocal praise of *A Portrait* spurred Joyce on to write more.

In March 1909 he wrote an article on Oscar Wilde for *Il Piccolo*. It gave him an opportunity to air one of his central obsessions: the artist as scapegoat. Wilde – an Irish genius surrounded by *amici indegni* ('unworthy friends') – had dared to defy the hypocritical piety of the rabblement and had been *esule e disonorata* ('exiled and dishonoured') by his country.[196] Joyce was grooming himself for a similar role. In April he sent *Dubliners* to another Dublin publisher, Maunsel & Co., and this time he decided to make his case in person.

In late July a gaunt, melancholy 27 year old arrived at Kingsdown pier, Dublin, holding his son's hand. *The first thing I saw on the pier*, Joyce told Nora in a postcard, *was Gogarty's fat back but I avoided him*.[197] He stayed with his family at 44 Fontenoy

A pacifist and a Jew, Ettore Schmitz (1861–1928) was one of Joyce's models for Leopold Bloom (and his wife, Livia Veneziani, inspired the name of Anna Livia Plurabelle in *Finnegans Wake*). Schmitz's first novels were poorly received, but *La coscienza di Zeno* (*Confessions of Zeno*, 1923) was hailed as a masterpiece, helped in part by Joyce's enthusiastic advocacy.

Street and John Joyce (despite his misgivings about Nora) was delighted to finally meet his grandson. Eileen thought her brother looked like a foreigner and everyone observed how much older and thinner he seemed.

Joyce's mission in Dublin was to get *Dubliners* published, but he was not averse to settling a few scores. He snubbed Gogarty in the street, but Gogarty ran after him and invited him home. *You have your life. Leave me to mine*, said Joyce. *You and I of 6 years ago are both dead. But I must write as I have felt.* According to Joyce, Gogarty replied '*I don't care a damn what you say of me so long as it is literature . . . Now will you shake hands with me at least?*' Joyce said *I will: on that understanding.*[198]

Joyce found George Roberts (the managing director of Maunsel & Co) *very self-important*, but *smoothed him down* and bought him a drink.[199] He could turn on the charm when he needed to and pointedly drank mineral water to scotch any rumours Roberts might have heard about his drinking. Roberts promised a verdict on *Dubliners* very soon.

Alert to threats and slights, Joyce was relieved to find most people friendly. He met the librarian W K Magee, George Russell and his old friends Kettle and Cosgrave. There were some exceptions: *I went to see Curran and found him looking ugly and disposed to be unfriendly.*[200] Byrne was pleased to see him and now lived at 7 Eccles Street, which Joyce would eventually make the address of Leopold Bloom. Joyce and Byrne rubbed along fairly well, but he spent most of his time drinking with Cosgrave. This proved a grave mistake.

Cosgrave let slip that he had gone out with Nora on those evenings when Joyce thought she was working at Finn's Hotel – Joyce's whole world fell apart. Nora, the only person he could trust, had betrayed him. He wrote a bitter, despairing letter to her: how could she be so disloyal, so dishonest, so cruel? How far had she gone with Cosgrave? Losing her meant losing love itself.

After a troubled night he wrote again with fresh allegations: *Is Georgie my son? . . . Perhaps they laugh when they see me parading 'my' son in the streets.*[201] He was at his most paranoid when he visited Byrne and wept openly at Nora's infidelity. The level-headed Byrne pointed out the obvious: Cosgrave was lying and had been put up to it by Gogarty. Nora had rebuffed Cosgrave's advances in 1904, when she was seeing Joyce, and Cosgrave had never forgotten.

Reassured, Joyce recovered his senses and sought to make amends: *My sweet noble Nora, I ask you to forgive me for my contemptible conduct but they maddened me, darling between them. We will defeat their cowardly plot, love. Forgive me, sweetheart, won't you?*[202]

On 19 August he signed a contract for *Dubliners* with Maunsel & Co, then went to Galway for the weekend with Giorgio. On the pretext of buying it, he entered the house where Nora had once lived with her grandmother so that he could see her bedroom. He stayed with her mother and discovered all he could about Nora's childhood. Cosgrave and Gogarty's vicious plot had failed: Joyce was more in love with Nora than ever.

How sick, sick, sick I am of Dublin! It is the city of failure, of rancour and of unhappiness. I long to be out of it.
Joyce to Nora, 1909[203]

Before leaving Dublin, he made several visits to the offices of the *Evening Telegraph* (details of which would one day appear in the 'Aeolus' episode of *Ulysses*). He and Byrne also took one last long walk around Dublin, revisiting their old haunts until 3 a.m. When they returned to 7 Eccles Street, Byrne had forgotten his key and had to climb over the railings to enter by a side door, just as Bloom would do in the 'Ithaca' episode.

Joyce left Dublin on the evening of 9 September, still smarting from Cosgrave's treachery. He took with him his sister, Eva, and a necklace for Nora. It consisted of five bone cubes – one for every year they had been together – and a plaque inscribed with the words *Love is unhappy when love is away* (a line from poem IX in *Chamber Music*). *It is dangerous to leave one's country,* Joyce confided to a friend in Trieste, *but still more dangerous to go back to it, for then your fellow-countrymen, if they can, will drive a knife into your heart.*[204]

Nevertheless, a month later he was in Dublin again, this time with a moneymaking scheme. He would provide Dublin with its first cinema. Backed by a syndicate of Triestine businessmen he found a suitable venue on Mary Street and staged a successful cinematographic exhibition there in December to attract publicity. It was a tense and miserable time. *I loathe Ireland and the Irish*, he told Nora. *They themselves stare at me in the street though I was born among them.*[206] Dublin made him paranoid and being separated from Nora for two and a half months didn't help: he began to doubt her loyalty all over again. Her letters reassured him and he talked his way into seeing Nora's room at Finn's Hotel to look at *the little bed in which a young girl had dreamed of me.*[207]

'It is a fact of crucial significance in the history of the novel this century that James Joyce opened the first cinema in Dublin in 1909. Joyce saw very early on that film must usurp some of the prerogatives which until then had belonged almost exclusively to the novelist.'
B S Johnson[205]

The so-called 'dirty' letters of December 1909 show how much he missed Nora, body and soul. Anyone who has read Bloom's adventures in the 'Circe' episode of *Ulysses* will not be surprised by the masochistic element in Joyce's letters. 'Circe' draws heavily on *Venus in Furs* (1870) by the Austrian novelist Leopold von Sacher-Masoch (1835–95); Joyce had several such books in his library and Nora liked them too. He had been brought up to associate sex with sin, but instead he found beauty where others saw filth. In his world the spiritual and the carnal happily coexist as essential aspects of the human condition. *I want you to read over and over all I have written to you*, he told Nora. *Some of it is ugly, obscene and bestial, some of it is pure and holy and spiritual: all of it is myself.*[208]

As soon as he had obtained a licence for the Volta Cinema, Joyce returned to Trieste on 1 January 1910, relieved to get *back to civilization* and to Nora.[209] He took with him another sister, Eileen, and before leaving Dublin he made one last attempt to sum himself up: *I am a poor impulsive sinful generous selfish jealous dissatisfied kind-natured poet.*[210]

Stanislaus was teaching at the Berlitz School, so Joyce took private pupils. His indolent, rather dissolute lifestyle annoyed his more responsible brother. They earned roughly the same from teaching, but Joyce squandered his money and leant heavily on Stanislaus for support. After a drinking binge in Pirano, Joyce suffered his first attack of iritis (an inflammation of the iris). He collapsed with the pain and spent the night and early morning lying in the street. It was a sign of more serious trouble ahead.

News came from Maunsel & Co in Dublin: they wanted him to tone down the language in 'Ivy Day in the Committee Room', especially a passage about the late King Edward VII's *bloody owl' mother*, Queen Victoria.[211] Joyce tinkered with it, but made few concessions. By July the Volta was losing money. His partners cut their losses and Joyce received a pittance for his efforts. Nothing seemed to be going right. Tired of supporting his brother's family, Stanislaus walked out and Joyce rowed with Nora. In a fit of petulance he flung the unfinished manuscript of *A Portrait* on the fire. Thankfully his sister Eileen rescued it.[212]

These were dark days indeed. With *Dubliners* stalled Joyce could not bring himself to work on *A Portrait*. In December he was still waiting for the proofs from Maunsel & Co, but the sticking point remained the reference to the King. Joyce waited and waited, until in July 1911 he threatened to take legal action for breach of contract. He even sent 'Ivy Day in the Committee Room' to Edward VII's son, George V, asking if he found it offensive. (His Majesty declined to comment.) In August, Joyce wrote an open letter to the Irish press protesting at the way he had been treated for seven years by so many Dublin publishers and quoting the disputed passage. Only two newspapers published it and it had no effect whatsoever.

Nora had been away from Ireland for eight years and was desperately homesick. In July 1912 she took Lucia to Dublin, before visiting her family in Galway. Joyce missed her terribly and, having heard no word from her after five days, set off in hot pursuit with Giorgio. Nora was pleased to see him and the whole family spent a relaxing three weeks in Galway. They also went to the Aran Islands, which Joyce wrote about with affection for *Il Piccolo*.

At this time foot and mouth in Ireland had made the British declare an embargo on Irish cattle and an Ulsterman friend in Trieste, Henry Blackwood Price, asked Joyce to seek out William Field, MP, the President of the Irish Cattle Traders' Society. Joyce helped to get an article by Price published in the *Evening Telegraph* (which is why Stephen mocks himself as *the bullockbefriending bard* in *Ulysses*).[213]

Meanwhile *Dubliners* was going nowhere. It had been set into type and printed, but the proofs languished at the printer's. Desperate to save his book, Joyce left Nora and the children in Galway and turned up at Maunsel & Co's offices in Dublin. George Roberts stood his ground: Joyce had to delete the reference to Edward VII and substitute fictitious names for all the shops and public houses he had mentioned to avoid libel; finally, he would have to remove 'An Encounter' from the collection.

Joyce was devastated. *I went into the backroom of the office* (he told Nora in a letter), *thinking of the book I have written, the child which I have carried for years and years in the womb of my imagination as you carried in your womb the children you love, and how I have fed it day after day out of my brain and my memory*.[214] He had no option but to agree to the new terms, provided *Dubliners* was published in the next two months.

The following day he spent a pleasant few hours at Maunsel & Co.'s offices discussing the paper, binding and advertisements for his book, but the next day Roberts decided not to publish *Dubliners* on legal advice. Joyce went for a long walk, *feeling the whole future of my life slipping out of my grasp.*[215] He even considered buying a revolver to *put some daylight into my publisher.*[216] But he would not give up. *I will fight to the last inch with every weapon in my power*, he told Stanislaus.[217] He pawned his watch and chain in order to buy more time to negotiate with Maunsel & Co, but to no avail. Roberts offered him the proofs of *Dubliners* for £30 and Joyce agreed, though he could ill afford it. He planned to publish it himself, but the printer had decided the book was anti-Irish and had destroyed the proofs. Joyce had nothing to show for his efforts. It was all over.

That was the last time he set foot on Irish soil. On 11 September 1912 Joyce left Dublin for ever. *I find it difficult to come to any other conclusion but this*, he said of his visit, *that the intention was to weary me out and if possible strangle me once and for all. But in this they did not succeed.*[218]

Litterarum Anglicarum Pontifex Maximus

Joyce didn't leave Dublin empty-handed: he brought back with him a copy of the *Evening Telegraph* for Thursday 16 June 1904, which he scrutinized for details – the Ascot Gold Cup race (won by Throwaway, an outsider), the excursion steamer *General Slocum* on fire, the Gordon Bennett Cup in Germany – that might lend his new novel verisimilitude. He also consulted the Dublin section of *Thom's Official Directory* (1904) in order to meticulously recreate a Dublin to which he would never return.

On the journey home he penned 'Gas from a Burner', a furious broadside which has a Dublin printer saying: *No, ladies, my press shall have no share in / So gross a libel on Stepmother Erin* [i.e. Ireland] . . . *I'll burn that book, so help me devil. / I'll sing a psalm as I watch it burn / And the ashes I'll keep in a one-handled urn* [i.e. a chamber pot].[220] It is a good example of Joyce embellishing the facts – the proofs were guillotined, not burned, but a martyr needs a bonfire. His brother Charles distributed the poem in Dublin.

I want to give a picture of Dublin so complete that if the city one day suddenly disappeared from the earth it could be reconstructed out of my book.
James Joyce[219]

In Trieste, Stanislaus had been left to deal with Joyce's irate landlord, who threatened the whole family with eviction. Wisely, he had moved their belongings into a smaller flat at 4 via Donato Bramante, near the cathedral of San Giusto. Joyce taught in the morning at the Scuola Superiore di Commercio Revoltella and gave private lessons in the afternoon. It was probably around this time that he became infatuated with one of his wealthy pupils. He was so bewitched by Amalia Popper that he made notes: *A pale*

face surrounded by heavy odorous furs. Her movements are shy and nerv-
ous . . . A skirt caught back by her sudden moving knee; a white lace edging
of an underskirt lifted unduly; a leg-stretched web of stocking . . .[221]

What this beautiful Triestene Jewess made of Signor Yoyce –
with his limp handshake and gangly frame, his eyes grotesquely
magnified behind thick lenses – we can probably guess. Joyce was
no longer young and he approaches his predicament with wistful
irony, aware of how ridiculous he must appear to her: *I rush out of*
the tobacco-shop and call her name. She turns and halts to hear my jum-
bled words of lessons, hours, lessons, hours: and slowly her pale cheeks are
flushed with a kindling opal light.[222] In the end he had to accept the
truth: *It will never be. You know that well. What then? Write it, damn*
you, write it! What else are you good for?[223] The result was *Giacomo*
Joyce, a confessional account of his feelings for this unattainable
ideal of womanhood. It also contains some of his most beautiful,
haunting descriptions of cities – Padua at night and Paris and
Trieste in the early morning – which are reminiscent of the prose
poems of Baudelaire or Rimbaud. Signorina Popper kept her distance, though she is thought to have inspired the poem 'A Flower
Given to My Daughter' and her father, Leopoldo, is a probable
source for Bloom's first name.[224]

In December 1912 Joyce sent *Dubliners* to the publisher Martin
Secker, but it was rejected. He would have to wait a whole year
for any sign that his prospects might change. In November 1913
he began work on a three-act play, *Exiles*, which he completed the
following May. Joyce could write dramatic fiction, but he was not
a natural dramatist. The themes of the play – a mother's death, a
son's elopement, a friend's betrayal, cuckoldry, the dilemma of
whether to settle in one's country and improve it or escape with
one's soul intact – are more successfully treated in *A Portrait* and
Ulysses, which was taking shape in Joyce's mind around this time.
Joyce identified with the hero, Richard Rowan, who has returned
to Dublin after nine years' exile with his common-law wife Bertha

and their child. Richard's oldest friend, a Dublin journalist called Robert Hand, propositions Bertha and the free thinking Richard gives her total freedom to follow her instincts. In the final act it is unclear whether she and Robert have become lovers, but Richard is tormented by *a deep wound of doubt which can never be healed*.[225]

There are aspects of Gogarty and Cosgrave in the character of Robert Hand, but the most important model was Roberto Prezioso, the editor of *Il Piccolo*. Joyce didn't object to his wife having an admirer and even encouraged Prezioso's afternoon visits to Nora (who would relay every detail of Prezioso's overtures for Joyce's entertainment). It was only when Prezioso tried to become Nora's lover (around 1911–12) that Joyce confronted his Italian rival, who quickly withdrew. This episode provided him with the plot for his play, which he likened to a game of cat-and-mouse. *Exiles* received favourable reviews when it was published in 1918 and many years later, in 1970, Harold Pinter's production at the Mermaid Theatre, London, was acclaimed as a major theatrical discovery.

In December 1913 Joyce received a letter from Ezra Pound (a friend of Yeats) who was to prove an important champion of his work. Pound would include *I hear an army charging upon the land* in *Des Imagistes* (1914), an anthology of Imagist verse. He was also connected with a maga-

'If Joyce owed a posthumous debt to Pinter, it was equally clear that Pinter was a living beneficiary of Joyce, not least in his preoccupation with the unverifiable nature of truth and the unpossessability of the female soul. The confluences of style and theme between the two writers were extraordinary; and working on Joyce's unclaimed masterpiece seemed to have a liberating effect on Pinter himself as a writer . . . He sat down to write *Old Times* in the winter of 1970 while saturated in Joyce's play . . . *Exiles* also planted seeds which were to germinate many years later in *Betrayal*.'
Michael Billington, *The Life and Work of Harold Pinter*[226]

zine called the *Egoist* whose editor, an Englishwoman named Harriet Shaw Weaver, was to play a crucial role in Joyce's life.

In January 1914, much to Joyce's surprise, Grant Richards changed his mind and offered to publish *Dubliners*. At the same time *A Portrait* began to be serialized in the *Egoist*. Small magazines came into their own during this period and it was largely through such publications as the *Egoist*, the *Little Review*, the *Criterion*, the *transatlantic review* and *transition* that many of the classic texts of Modernism first found an audience. At the forefront of modern taste, these magazines were a crucial part of the literary scene at a time when there was an unprecedented explosion in

Benefactress: Harriet Shaw Weaver

experimental literature. Without them, many new writers such as Joyce would never have seen their defiantly uncommercial works in print.

After a delay of nine years, the publication of *Dubliners* caused little fuss. The reviews were mediocre, except for Ezra Pound's in the *Egoist*. He praised Joyce's 'clear hard prose' and admired the way he wrote about real life without forcing it into the conventional form of a story ('Araby', for instance, he described as 'a vivid waiting') – here was a new kind of Irish writer: unsentimental, rigorous, realist and uncontaminated by 'the Irish or "Celtic" imagination'.[227] *Dubliners* marked a new phase in Irish literature, but for Joyce its publication had come too late. He had written it between the ages of 22 and 25, but he was now 32 and attracting admiration as the author of *A Portrait*.

Austria-Hungary declared war on Serbia in July 1914 and the First World War began. Despite the erratic wartime postal system, Joyce continued to send chapters of *A Portrait* to the *Egoist*. He had originally planned to end his fictional autobiography with his elopement with Nora, but decided instead to finish with his symbolic flight to Paris in 1902. Stephen's last diary entry is a prayer to Daedalus: *Old father, old artificer, stand me now and ever in good stead.*[228] The next time we meet Stephen, in *Ulysses*, he has returned to Dublin and is living with Mulligan in the Martello tower, brooding on his mother's death.

In July or August 1914 – poised between completing *A Portrait* and beginning *Ulysses* – Joyce wrote the final version of *Giacomo Joyce* in his best handwriting on eight large sheets of heavy art paper. He had no intention of publishing such a personal document, but he borrowed and adapted whole sections of *Giacomo Joyce* for use in the last chapter of *A Portrait* and later in *Ulysses*. Giacomo is a sort of missing link between the young Stephen and the middle-aged Bloom, and his introspective, first-person narrative anticipates the stream of consciousness technique of *Ulysses*.

By November 1914 Joyce was hard at work on the novel that would make him famous. *Ulysses* was to be *a continuation of* A Portrait of the Artist as a Young Man *after three years' interval blended with many of the persons of* Dubliners.[229] He made notes for the novel *on stray bits of paper which I then forget in the most unlikely places, in books, under ornaments and in my pockets and on the back of advertisements.*[230] In a *halting, meditative manner*, Joyce deciphered these with the aid of a magnifying glass, then wove them into his narrative, crossing them off as he went.[231] So began the slow, laborious process of composition.

In January 1915 Stanislaus was arrested as a spy for visiting some fortifications in Trieste and spent the rest of the War in an

Joyce the dandy: photographed by Ottocaro Weiss, Zurich, 1915

Austrian detention centre. Joyce took on Stanislaus's pupils at the language school and also accepted a part-time job as English correspondent for a paint factory. By April he had almost finished *Exiles*, but in May, when Italy entered the war, Trieste was partially evacuated. As an enemy alien Joyce could either leave or be interned. He abandoned his furniture and books (and the manuscript of *Giacomo Joyce*) and in late June took his family to Zurich. They were back at the Gasthaus Hoffnung, where Joyce and Nora had arrived 11 years before. A succession of tiny flats followed until they finally came to rest at 54 Seefeldstrasse.

Without Stanislaus or the Berlitz School, Joyce's financial situation was desperate. Nevertheless, through the efforts of Pound and others he was gaining a reputation as an important literary figure. He accepted a £75 grant from the Royal Literary Fund and he was famous enough to receive an entry form for *Who's Who* (1916) on which, under 'Recreations', he wrote *Singing*.

Joyce took on a few language pupils, but was practically unemployed. He stayed out late in cafés and rose late in the morning, though he continued to work *Ulysses. If I could find out in the meantime who is the patron of men of letters I should try to remind him that I exist*, he joked to Nora's uncle Michael Healy in November 1915, *but I understand that the last saint who held that position resigned in despair and no other will take the portfolio.*[232]

Founded in 1790 the Royal Literary Fund is the oldest and largest charity serving literature. It was set up to help writers who have fallen on hard times through illness, family misfortune or other hardships.

Many refugees gathered in neutral Zurich, among them a group of radical new artists. 'Revolted by the butchery of the 1914 World War, we in Zurich devoted ourselves to the arts,' recalled one of them, Hans Arp. 'While the guns rumbled in the distance, we sang, painted, made collages and wrote poems with all our might.'[233] Joyce was certainly aware of the Dadaists, though it is hard to say how much their experimental language games influenced the direction of *Ulysses*.

Dadaism was anti-art and anti-sense. Its main protagonists were Hugo Ball (1886–1927), Hans Arp (1887–1966), Hans Richter (1888–1976), Richard Huelsenbeck (1892–1974) and Tristan Tzara (1896–1963). After the war, Dada moved on to Paris where it merged with Surrealism, while Marcel Duchamp (1887–1968) exported it to the United States.

The final instalment of *A Portrait* appeared in the *Egoist* in September 1915 and Joyce was eager to see it become a book. Duckworth's reader, Edward Garnett (who had turned down D H Lawrence's *The Rainbow* in 1914), rejected it as 'too discursive, formless, unrestrained, and ugly things, ugly words, are too prominent'.[234] In November the prosecution of the publishers of *The Rainbow* for obscenity meant that nobody would touch Joyce's new novel. Fortunately he had a small subsidy from the Society of Authors and in August 1916 he was awarded a Civil List grant of

£100 by Herbert Henry Asquith (1852–1928), the British Prime Minister (Joyce's contempt for the British Empire did not prevent him from accepting it). In December 1916, at long last, B W Huebsch in New York published *A Portrait of the Artist as a Young Man* and *Dubliners* in the United States.

More good news came in February 1917. An anonymous benefactor offered to send him £200 a year for as long as the war lasted. Joyce had no idea who it might be, but he was glad of the money. In that same month, Miss Weaver published a British edition of *A Portrait* under the imprint of The Egoist Press. One English reviewer declared that 'no clean-minded person could possibly allow it to remain within reach of his wife, his sons or daughters' and H G Wells complained of Joyce's 'cloacal obsession . . . If the reader is squeamish upon these matters, then there is nothing for it but to shun this book.'[235]

Once again Pound came to the rescue. He admired Joyce's 'clear-cut and definite sentences' and defended him against the charge of being sordid. *A Portrait* was full of 'shabbiness, squalor, and sordidness', admittedly, but there were also passages of great beauty and 'There is no perception of beauty without a corresponding disgust.'[236] Pound assumed that Joyce shared his

> *As regards* Ulysses *I write and think and write and think all day and part of the night. It goes on as it has been going these five or six years. But the ingredients will not fuse until they have reached a certain temperature.*
>
> Joyce to Ezra Pound, July 1917[237]

distaste for the sordid, but this was far from the case. As he says in one of the 'dirty' letters to Nora, sometimes the dirtiest words are the most beautiful.

Joyce's eyes grew worse and in August he was in such pain he couldn't move. It was glaucoma, a debilitating eye disease and a common cause of blindness. His doctor advised him to spend the winter in the Swiss town of Locarno. Nora and the children went first, but before Joyce could leave he had another painful attack.

There was no choice but to operate, a frightening prospect for anyone, but especially terrifying for a writer. After an iridectomy on his right eye he was totally blind for three days and suffered a nervous collapse. Nora returned to comfort him and in October they finally escaped to the milder climate of Locarno.

Joyce was unable to read or write for some time, but in Locarno he finally finished the first three episodes of *Ulysses* (the Telemachia). He had them typed and sent to Pound who replied 'Wall, Mr Joice, I recon your a damn fine writer . . . An' I recon' this here work o' yourn is some concarn'd litterchure.'[238] The *Little Review* began serialization in March the following year.

Joyce found other diversions in Locarno: he became enamoured of Gertrude Kaempffer, a 26-year-old doctor. He lent her *Chamber Music* and *A Portrait* and made his feelings known, but she kept him at a distance and destroyed his letters. He was left with just his fantasies, but perhaps Gertrude lingers on in the character of Gerty MacDowell in *Ulysses*.

A thunderstorm persuaded him to cut short his three-month stay and return to Zurich in early January 1918 (his lifelong terror of thunderstorms was a leftover of his Catholic boyhood, when his pious governess had taught him to cross himself and pray whenever lightning flashed). Joyce and his family moved into a new flat at 38 Universitätstrasse. Above his writing desk hung a photograph of his friend Ettore Schmitz and another of a Greek statue of Penelope, Ulysses's wife.

In February he received news of another anonymous benefactor. Edith Rockefeller McCormick (who supported several writers and artists in Zurich, as well as the psychoanalyst Carl Jung) offered him a monthly allowance of 1,000 Swiss francs. With money in the bank Joyce dropped some of his pupils and dedicated himself to *Ulysses* and the Zurich cafés, where he spent most evenings deep in conversation with Frank Budgen, an English artist and writer.

Dining out: Joyce, Nora, Lucia and Giorgio, Zurich 1915

Zurich was an important theatrical centre and Joyce now found himself involved in a plan to set up a company to perform plays in English. As the business manager of The English Players, he went to the British Consulate to ask for its official blessing. The consul-general, a man named Bennett, offered his support, though he was suspicious of Joyce. Bennett had sent him an invitation to register for military service, which Joyce had quickly returned as addressed to him in error. Bennett also probably knew of Joyce's poem 'Dooleysprudence', an anti-war satire in which the pacifist Mr Dooley pours scorn on all belligerent nations.

Joyce hoped The English Players might eventually perform *Exiles*, but their first play was Oscar Wilde's *The Importance of Being Earnest* (1895). He threw himself into the project and hand-picked the cast. Henry Carr, a former British soldier who worked at the British Consulate was given the lead role of Algernon Moncrieff, for which he bought a pair of trousers, gloves and a hat. Carr disliked Joyce and the feeling was mutual. Nevertheless, the performance was a success and as the audience applauded

Joyce shouted *Hurrah for Ireland! Poor Wilde was Irish and so am I!*[239]

Afterwards all hell broke loose. Carr asked to be reimbursed for the cost of his costume, but Joyce refused: Carr would wear the items in question long after the play closed, he argued, and Carr actually owed the Players money for some tickets he had sold. Carr called him a cad and a swindler and threatened to throw him downstairs. Joyce demanded that Bennett dismiss Carr from his job, but Bennett sided with Carr. Joyce's attitude to the British hardened: he looked forward to Germany winning the war. When he sued Carr for the money owed and for libel the judge found in his favour and Carr had to pay court costs and Joyce's expenses.

It was a victory of sorts, but for as long as they kept Joyce as their business manager, Bennett made life difficult for The English Players. Joyce appealed to Sir Horace Rumbold, the British Minister to Bern, but without success. Rumbold had been informed by the consul-general that 'Mr Joyce and his company are the most undesirable people and their performances are very mediocre and are neither socially nor professionally in the interests of British propaganda.'[240] In fact, the British authorities so disliked Joyce that they even considered revoking his British passport. In the end Joyce withdrew from the Players so that the show could go on, but he got his revenge. At first, Rumbold became *Sir Whorearse Rumphole* in Joyce's letters, then in *Ulysses* he is *H Rumbold, Master Barber*, who offers his services as a hangman; he is also an aspect of the evil Ondt in *Finnegans Wake* (*raumybult*).[241] Carr turns up in *Ulysses* as one of the soldiers who attacks Stephen. His sergeant major is Bennett.

In May 1918 Joyce was once again brought low by an attack of iritis, but he was pleased when *Exiles* was published in Britain and the United States. Meanwhile *Ulysses* continued to appear in instalments in the *Little Review* and it has been suggested that Joyce might have written a very different a novel had it not been for the pressure of serial publication. Was Joyce merely showing

off to his American readers when he decided to make each suc-
ceeding episode a virtuoso performance? Whatever the case, the
'Sirens' episode, which he began working on that year, marks a
clear turning point. 'Without the intruded fragments of tedious
word-play,' one critic has observed, 'it would have been one of the
best scenes in the old vein . . . But we are fidgeted by all that
feeble, pre-*Finnegan* word-play.'[242]

In December 1918 Joyce had another attack of love at first
sight. This time the object of his attentions was Martha
Fleischmann, a dark-haired Swiss woman who lived just around
the corner from him. The bored mistress of an engineer, she was
flattered by Joyce's attentions. He sent her secret notes in French
and German, though whether their relationship was ever con-
summated is open to question. Eventually she confessed everything to her engineer. Joyce received a threatening letter and had
to go round to smooth things over.

He justified his infidelity (as he did his drinking) by claiming
that, as an artist, it would be *spiritual death* for him not to follow
his inclinations.[243] He might even have stage-managed the affair
with Martha to generate ideas for his novel. He was not averse to
inventing such situations and Nora once complained to a mutual
friend, 'Jim wants me to go with other men so that he will have
something to write about.'[244] In a postcard, Joyce referred to
Martha as 'Nausicaa' and to himself as 'Odysseus'. She had a limp,
as does Gerty MacDowell ('Nausicaa' in *Ulysses*). Also, in his letters to Martha, Joyce signed his name with Greek 'e's, just as
Bloom does in his clandestine correspondence with Martha
Clifford (in 'Lotus Eaters'). Miss Clifford hopes to meet her
naughty boy one day, but she will be disappointed.[245] Bloom does
not want an affair, he just likes to be titillated and plans to gradually spice up his letters to her.

At Nora's request, Joyce consented to drink wine rather than
absinthe. The green fairy had been a faithful companion for many

Writing *Ulysses*, Zurich 1919

years and he refused to drink red wine because of its Eucharistic overtones. In the end he settled for a Swiss white, which tasted, he said, like an archduchess's urine. Meanwhile the unpleasant business with The English Players had not gone away. A second lawsuit followed and this time Carr won. Joyce refused to pay damages and the court opened proceedings against him. Fortunately his mysterious benefactor took this moment to send him £5,000, so he easily stumped up the 50 francs required to settle the matter.

In July 1919 he finally discovered the identity of his anonymous patron: it was Harriet Shaw Weaver, the editor of the *Egoist*. At the same time he received a letter from her saying that the 'Sirens' episode had been a disappointment. He was now writing every episode in a new style and 'Sirens' is all about the seductive power of music (alluding to the song of the sirens that deprives men of their senses in the *Odyssey*). It begins with a prelude and follows the structure of a fugue, but Miss Weaver was uncertain about this radical departure. If she didn't like 'Sirens', thought Joyce, what would she make of the next instalments, 'Cyclops' or 'Circe', which were to be even more experimental?

Pound also objected to 'Sirens', in particular Bloom's fart (*Pprrpffrrppfff*) at the end of the episode.[246] It isn't just a fart, however, it is an ironic commentary on the martyred patriot Robert Emmet's last words, which Bloom is reading in an antique-shop window at the same time. Emmet was a hero for Irish republicans and the idea of a blood sacrifice to achieve independence appealed to the leaders of the Easter Rising (in 'Cyclops', for instance, the Citizen talks of *Robert Emmet and die for your country*).[247] Joyce, on the other hand, in his Italian article on Fenianism, had referred to Emmet's 1803 rebellion against the British as a *rivolta ridicola* ('ridiculous revolt') and he parodies *the hero martyr's* execution in *Ulysses*.[248] When asked if he would lay down his life for Ireland, Joyce replied *let Ireland die for me* and in *Ulysses* Stephen is of the same opinion.[249]

In August *Exiles* had its premiere (in German) in Munich. Joyce declared it *A fiasco!* and it lasted only one performance.[250] Zurich bored him now and he longed to return to Trieste, but before leaving he received some bad news: Edith McCormick had cancelled his monthly stipend. No explanation was given, though it is possible the psychoanalyst Carl Jung had told her Joyce was an alcoholic. Joyce had refused to be psychoanalysed by Jung, whom he referred to as Tweedledum to Freud's Tweedledee.

The Easter Rising (1916) was an armed revolt against the British government. Patrick Pearse, the leader of the IRB, and James Connolly with his Citizen Army proclaimed the establishment of the Irish Republic. After serious street fighting in Dublin, the rebel leaders were rounded up and executed.

Joyce and his family arrived in Trieste in October. He retrieved his furniture, books and papers from storage and they all moved in with Stanislaus and another family at 2 via Sanità. Relations between the brothers had cooled considerably. Stanislaus had been four years in a prison camp, whereas Joyce, when asked how he had spent the war years, liked to reply airily, *Oh yes, I was told that there was a war going on in Europe.*[251]

He read and wrote nothing for six weeks after arriving in Trieste, but eventually began work on 'Nausicaa', in which Bloom becomes aroused while spying on a young girl on Sandymount Strand. Because Bloom assumes Gerty MacDowell's head is full of romance fiction, fashion magazine clichés and advertising slogans, the entire episode is written in *a namby-pamby jammy marmalady drawersy (alto là!) style*.[252] He lent it to Stanislaus, who dismissed it as a joke, but Miss Weaver proved more perceptive and came close to the truth about him: 'though you are neither priest nor doctor of medicine, I think you have something of both.'[253]

Encouraged, Joyce began 'Oxen of the Sun', probably the most ambitious episode of *Ulysses*. The action takes place around 10 p.m. at the Holles Street Maternity Hospital. Mrs Purefoy has been in labour for three days and is about to give birth to her ninth child, Mortimer. Bloom asks after Mrs Purefoy (whom he has been worrying about all day) and is invited to join a party of medical students and their friends, including a rather drunk Stephen. The young men grow increasingly rowdy, though there is a moment of calm reflection when the baby is born. Stephen suggests they move on to Burke's pub, where the drinking continues until closing time (everyone drinks absinthe, except Bloom who sips red wine);[254] they then head for the brothel district.

The plot is quite straightforward, but in keeping with the theme of birth and gestation the narrative style proceeds through the entire history of English prose from its origins to the modern day. After a short Latinate prelude, the language develops from a rudimentary Anglo-Saxon rhythm through to the more elaborate prose of the Middle Ages, the sophistication of the Elizabethans, the Augustans and the Victorians *until it ends in a frightful jumble of Pidgin English, nigger English, Cockney, Irish, Bowery slang and broken doggerel*.[255] As the absinthe hits home, the narrative becomes largely unintelligible, anticipating the style of *Finnegans Wake*. Joyce overcame considerable difficulties in 'Oxen of the Sun', which is divided into nine sections corresponding to the nine-month gestation period of the foetus. An exhilarated T S Eliot read it as symbolic of 'the futility of all the English styles' and this was perhaps Joyce's aim, for as he told Miss Weaver, *each successive episode, dealing with some province of artistic culture (rhetoric or music or dialectic), leaves behind it a burnt up field.*[256] This is one reason why *Ulysses* is regarded as a singular landmark in the history of the novel. After Joyce, there was no going back.

By May he was tired of Trieste. Before the war it had been a busy port of the Austro-Hungarian Empire, but now it was a dull, provincial Italian city. He wanted to be at the centre of things and a visit to Ezra Pound in Sirmione set him on a new course. Pound persuaded him he should live in London, where he would be nearer Dublin and his father. In July 1920 Joyce turned over his teaching job to Stanislaus and set about *wheeling the caravan of my family* out of Trieste.[257] They passed through Venice, Milan, Dijon and rested in Paris, where they planned to stay for a week.

In Paris, Pound had worked his magic. He had distributed copies of *A Portrait* to influential friends and found Joyce rooms in a hotel on the rue de l'Université. By the time the 38-year-old Joyce arrived, he was already the talk of the town among the Paris literati. On 11 July Pound introduced him to Sylvia Beach, a young American who owned a bookshop on the Left Bank called Shakespeare & Company at 8 rue Dupuytren. Joyce wrote the name in a notebook and turned up the next day wearing a dark blue serge suit, a black felt hat and dirty tennis shoes. Almost immediately Shakespeare & Company became his unofficial press office. Beach and her friend Adrienne Monnier (who owned a bookshop called La Maison des Amis des Livres at 12 rue de l'Odéon) enthusiastically recommended his work to their British and American customers. Joyce welcomed the attention and it was gratifying to discover that those in the know rated him as highly as he rated himself.

He soon became something of a legend and liked to recount the stories he had heard about himself: James Joyce was a spy working for Austria or Britain; he was dying in New York; he was a cocaine fiend; a Sinn Féin emissary in Switzerland; a violent

Image-conscious: with Sylvia Beach at Shakespeare & Co

Bolshevik propagandist; the lover of a princess; the owner of several cinemas; and the founder of Dadaism. Best of all was the rumour that *Ulysses was a prearranged pro-German code.*[258]

In August he was visited by T S Eliot and Wyndham Lewis, who observed that Joyce wore 'patent-leather shoes, large powerful spectacles, and a small gingerbread beard . . . playing the Irishman a little overmuch perhaps, but in amusingly mannered technique.'[259] By nature shy, Joyce hid behind an exaggerated politeness, which Eliot interpreted as arrogance; nevertheless it was Eliot who did most to promote Joyce in Britain. Joyce was less certain of Eliot's gifts until he read *The Waste Land* (1922), which he admired enough to parody in *Finnegans Wake*.

Joyce was besieged by visitors and invitations, but the novelty soon wore off and as his fame increased he became more reserved.

He was tired of being *cooped up in overcrowded rooms listening to gossip about absent artists and replying to enthusiastic expressions about my (unread) masterpiece with a polite amused reflective smile.*[260] Only *Ulysses* really interested him and he hoped to finish 'Circe' before Christmas.

On 21 September he wrote a letter to the Italian translator Carlo Linati in which, for the first time, he drew up a chart to explain the complex structure of *Ulysses*. Here, in translation, is Joyce's summary:

It is the epic of two races (Israel–Ireland) and at the same time the cycle of the human body as well as a little story of a day (life). The character of Ulysses has fascinated me ever since boyhood. I started writing a short story for Dubliners *fifteen years ago but gave it up. For seven years I have been working at this book – blast it! It is also a kind of encyclopedia. My intention is not only to render the myth* sub specie temporis nostri *['according to the mood of our times'] but also to allow each adventure (that is, every hour, every organ, every art being interconnected and interrelated in the somatic scheme of the whole) to condition and even to create its own technique. Each adventure is so to speak one person although it is composed of persons.*[261]

In early December, with a little help from his friends, Joyce moved into an expensive property on the Boulevard Raspail. *Is it not extraordinary*, he wrote to Budgen, *the way I enter a city barefoot and end up in a luxurious flat.*[262] Just before Christmas he completed the 'Circe' episode, having rewritten it nine times. He thought it the best thing he had ever done. By February 1921 'Eumaeus' was with the typist, but the question remained: who would publish *Ulysses*?

British printers would not touch it and the US Post Office had confiscated and destroyed several issues of the *Little Review* after a complaint from the Society for the Prevention of Vice that the 'Nausicaa' episode of *Ulysses* was pornographic. The editors – Margaret Anderson and Jane Heap – had been convicted of publishing obscenity and ordered to pay a $50 fine. *Ulysses* was officially banned in the United States and remained so for another twelve years. In March, B W Huebsch (who had published *A Portrait* and *Dubliners* in America) reluctantly informed Joyce he could not accept his new novel without substantial changes. Joyce complained to Sylvia Beach at her Paris bookshop and she came up with an unusual idea: why not publish *Ulysses* under the imprint of Shakespeare & Company?

How could Joyce refuse? The terms were excellent and he agreed to an unheard of 66 per cent royalty. The print run was 1,000 copies, some printed on expensive paper and signed by the author. Among those who expressed an interest in *Ulysses* were Yeats, André Gide (1869–1951), Ernest Hemingway (1899–1961) and even the British Minister of War, Winston Churchill (1875–1965).

The French writer Valéry Larbaud (1881–1957), a drinking companion and champion of Joyce's work, offered him his flat rent-free for the summer and the family moved to 71 rue du Cardinal Lemoine in June. Meanwhile Joyce's benefactor, Miss Weaver, had challenged him in a letter on his alcoholic excess. He asked friends to reassure her that Mr Joyce drank, but in moderation and merely to relax. The fact is, drinking released something in him: he would quote poetry (usually Verlaine or Dante) and was well known in the Paris bars as *le poète*.

In late May 1921 a mild attack of iritis presaged more trouble ahead. The first proofs of *Ulysses* arrived in June and from his notes Joyce made thousands of changes (like Proust, he was a publisher's nightmare) until the book grew a third in size. He was still sending emendations and corrections a week before it was published. The strain took its toll and by July his eyes were so bad he took cocaine to relieve the pain. That month Larbaud returned and the Joyces moved back to the rue de l'Université. By then the final episode, 'Penelope', was with the printers, which is just as well as Larbaud planned to lecture on *Ulysses* in December.

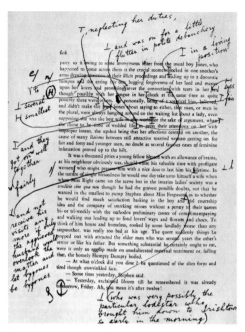

Last -minute changes: *Ulysses*

'Ithaca' was the last section to be completed and Joyce sent Larbaud another scheme of *Ulysses, in order to help him to confuse the audience a little more.*[263]

Obfuscation was one of Joyce's strategies for acquiring lasting fame, as was his decision never to challenge the numerous, often conflicting interpretations of *Ulysses*. All publicity was good publicity. When asked by the French translator of *Ulysses* for some kind of scheme of the book, Joyce was generally uncooperative. *If I gave it all up immediately*, he explained, *I'd lose my immortality. I've put in so many enigmas and puzzles that it will keep the professors busy for centuries arguing over what I meant, and that's the only way of insuring one's immortality.*[264] No summary can do justice to the scope of *Ulysses*, and Joyce even introduced into his book material that will always remain a mystery. For instance, it was a favourite game of his to ask friends to guess *Who was the man in the mackintosh?*[265]

Joyce placed great emphasis on birthdays and, at his request, Shakespeare & Company published *Ulysses* on his fortieth, 2 February 1922. Joyce, Nora, and their friends celebrated that evening at an Italian restaurant, where Joyce finally unwrapped the parcel containing his copy of *Ulysses* (delivered by taxi by Sylvia Beach). He had spent 16 years thinking about it and seven years writing it: at last he had a copy in his hands. The book's design was his: white letters on a blue background, which suggested to him a white island rising from the sea. He took great delight in pointing out to his friends that their names were in the book, an important impulse for Joyce.

In Dublin, meanwhile, people worriedly asked 'Am I in it?'

The Blue Book of Eccles

The plot of *Ulysses* is simple. Any difficulties for the reader arise more from the style than the content. It deals with the events of a single day in Dublin, Thursday 16 June 1904 (the day he first walked out with Nora), from 8 a.m. to 2 a.m., and follows the adventures of Stephen Dedalus, lately back from Paris, and a middle-aged Irish Jew, Leopold Bloom. In the last episode, we drop in on the thoughts of his wife, Marion (Molly) Bloom (née Tweedy).

Joyce's unique turn of mind allowed him to see parallels of all kinds between Homer's *Odyssey* and the story he wanted to tell. He regarded Ulysses as the best kind of male role model: he was a son (to Laertes), a father (to Telemachus), a husband (to Penelope), a lover (to Calypso), a warrior at Troy, a voyager and King of Ithaca. In short, he was *a complete man . . . a good man*.[266] In the Homeric parallel, Bloom is Ulysses, Molly is Penelope and Stephen is their 'son', Telemachus. In Trieste Joyce had drafted the first three episodes, which deal with Stephen, but in Zurich he turned his attention to Ulysses himself.

Leopold Bloom is Joyce's most enduring creation. In appearance he is nothing special, though he

Bloomsday (16 June) is celebrated around the world. In Dublin, Joyce pilgrims retrace Leopold Bloom's itinerary: *grilled mutton kidneys* for breakfast; at lunchtime *a light snack in Davy Byrne's* pub (21 Duke Street) consisting of a Gorgonzola sandwich with mustard and *a glass of burgundy*; in the afternoon, *Liver and bacon*, *mashed potatoes* and *gravy* and a pint of *cool stout* at the Ormond Hotel (8 Upper Ormond Quay).[267] Bloomsday in Dublin attracts thousands of people a year and includes readings, re-enactments, music, theatre, street performances, James Joyce look-alike contests and great quantities of Guinness.

Privately, Joyce gave Homeric titles to the 18 episodes of *Ulysses*, but they do not appear in the book, nor are they numbered:

Part I (the *Telemachia*)
(1) Telemachus (8 a.m.)
(2) Nestor (10 a.m.)
(3) Proteus (11 a.m.)

Part II (the *Odyssey*)
(1) Calypso (8 a.m.)
(2) Lotus Eaters (10 a.m.)
(3) Hades (11 a.m.)
(4) Aeolus (12 noon)
(5) Lestrygonians (1 p.m.)
(6) Scylla and Charybdis (2 p.m.)
(7) Wandering Rocks (3 p.m.)
(8) Sirens (4 p.m.)
(9) Cyclops (5 p.m.)
(10) Nausicaa (8 p.m.)
(11) Oxen of the Sun (10 p.m.)
(12) Circe (midnight)

Part III (the *Nostos* or 'Return Home')
(1) Eumaeus (1 a.m.)
(2) Ithaca (2 a.m.)
(3) Penelope (infinity)

is never fully described. 'Nowhere is it stated that Bloom was balding, plump, moustached, soft-eyed or full-lipped,' observes the artist Richard Hamilton, 'and neither his carriage nor his demeanour are defined; yet portrayals of him, whether in artists' illustrations or casting on stage, film and TV, all reveal the same archetype.'[268] Joyce made a pencil sketch of Bloom in which he wears a bowler hat, has a round head, a broad moustache and slanted, *largelidded eyes*.[269] We also know that Bloom is *five feet nine inches and a half* and weighs *eleven stone and four pounds*, that his collar size is 17 and his waistcoat has five buttons.[270] One of his enemies refers to his *dunducketymudcoloured mug* and we can assume he is a rather unprepossessing figure by the way others treat him.[271] He is respected by a few, reviled by many, but much of the time either ignored or merely tolerated. Those who are friendly to his face ridicule him behind his back, whether it be his flat-footed walk, his foreignness or the widely known fact that his wife is unfaithful. Once *a traveller for blottingpaper* with Wisdom Hely's, he now *does some canvassing for ads* (like C P McCoy in the short story 'Grace').[272]

Joyce had already written a novel about Stephen Dedalus and by the time he came to write *Ulysses* he was much less interested in this version of his younger self (now 22 in *Ulysses*). The 38-year-old Leopold Bloom is a more complete man in Joyce's eyes. Like Ulysses he is a son (to Rudolph), a father (to Milly and the deceased Rudy), a husband (to Molly) and a lover (his Henry Flower alter-ego). He might not be an intellectual like Stephen, but his interests are broader. He has a practical mind (always calculating how to save money or make a profit) and a layman's interest in science (always thinking of ways to improve the world), but he also dabbles in

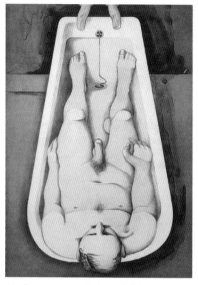

He foresaw his pale body (1990) Richard Hamilton's view of Bloom

theology and literature. *He's a cultured allroundman, Bloom is*, says Lenehan. *There's a touch of the artist about old Bloom.*[273]

Bloom is generally depicted as being kinder and gentler than the people he meets. An outsider, his greatest fear is causing offence. Temperamentally unqualified to join in the manly banter around him, when he does open his mouth he invariably strikes the wrong note. Joyce always divides men into two groups: the *womanly* men and the gallants.[274] Fastidious, thoughtful, sensitive men like Bloom or Stephen or Little Chandler (in *Dubliners*) often get hurt when they run up against coarse, macho men like Molly's lover 'Blazes' Boylan, 'Buck' Mulligan (Gogarty) or Ignatius Gallaher. Bloom is *the meekest man and the kindest* and in the end it is his humanity and gentleness that triumph, his faith in the power of love.[275]

Joyce saw more similarities than differences between the Irish and the Jews. They were both irrational, imaginative and impulsive and shared a similar history of *dispersal, persecution, survival and revival.*[276] (He also subscribed to a theory current at the time that the *Odyssey* was Semitic rather than Greek in origin.) In *Ulysses*, Stephen and Bloom discuss these *points of contact*, compare the ancient Hebrew and Irish languages and contemplate the prospects of national revival.[277]

Bloom's Jewishness sets him apart and he is a victim of racism. The worst misunderstanding occurs when Bantam Lyons thinks Bloom has given him a tip for the Ascot Gold Cup. Throwaway is the name of a horse in the race, but Bloom simply means he was about to throw away his newspaper. As it happens Throwaway wins and the mistaken belief that Bloom has secretly made £5 on the race infuriates his fellow Dubliners, who all backed a different horse. This provides them with an excuse to vent their anti-Semitism.

Bloom's loose definition of a nation as *the same people living in the same place* cuts no ice with the fierce nationalists in Barney Kiernon's pub.[278] Bloom claims Ireland as his nation, but he also belongs *to a race . . . that is hated and persecuted.*[279] No matter how much he tries to fit in, he will always be regarded as a *bloody jewman.*[280] In his most important speech, Joyce's pacifist principles come to the fore: *But it's no use*, says Bloom. *Force, hatred, history, all that. That's not life for men and women, insult and hatred. And everybody knows that it's the very opposite of that that is really life.*

—*What? says Alf.*

—*Love, says Bloom. I mean the opposite of hatred.*[281]

Bloom keeps such a low profile in Dublin that many are surprised to discover he is Molly's husband. She is a flamboyant and beautiful concert singer, though a little past her prime. Their marriage has lost its spark, however, and they have not had full intercourse for *10 years, 5 months and 18 days*, the last time being 27 November 1893.[282] (The sexually frustrated Bloom is reminded of this, on a subconscious level, by an advert in the

Freeman's Journal: What is home without Plumtree's Potted Meat? Incomplete. With it an abode of bliss.)[283] Molly gave birth to a son, Rudy, on 29 December 1893, but he died 11 days later and they were *never the same* afterwards.[284] Bloom has bottled up his grief and mourns inwardly, without causing a fuss, for the son he has lost: *If little Rudy had lived. See him grow up. Hear his voice in the house. Walking beside Molly in an Eton suit. My son.*[285]

Their daughter, Millicent (Milly), turned 15 the day before (15 June) and Bloom reads a letter from her in the morning. She is learning photography at Mullingar and he worries that the young student she talks about might take advantage. He is right: Milly is the *Photo girl* mentioned in the 'Telemachus' episode. *Snapshot, eh?* leers Mulligan. *Brief exposure.*[286]

Bloom cannot accompany his wife on her next concert tour as he has *some private business* to attend to: it is the anniversary of his father's death.[287] Rudolph Virag (who came from Hungary and anglicized his name to 'Bloom') committed suicide at the Queen's Hotel, Ennis, on 27 June 1886 by taking aconite poison. Bloom remembers the details of the case and keeps a letter in a drawer at home addressed *To My Dear Son Leopold.*[288] Phrases from his father's suicide note steal up on him throughout the day. In 'Hades', Jack Power unwittingly wounds Bloom by commenting on the disgrace of a suicide in the family and Martin Cunningham tries to smooth things over.[289]

A local lothario, Hugh 'Blazes' Boylan, is Molly's business manager and will accompany her on the coming tour. Bloom has good reason to be worried. Boylan will visit Molly at 4 p.m. to discuss the programme and Bloom is tortured all day by the thought of them having sex. *I could go home still*, he thinks around noon, but he doesn't.[290] To make matters worse, he catches glimpses of Boylan throughout the morning and early afternoon and his watch stops at precisely the hour when Molly sleeps with Boylan for the first time.

Bloom can justify his wife's infidelity on a number of levels and suspects her of sleeping with a long list of others, but his matter-of-factness cannot disguise his anguish and jealousy. In the dream world of the 'Circe' episode he becomes a eunuch, a cuckold whose antlered head Boylan uses as a hatstand. Just as Bloom's decade of celibacy mirrors Ulysses's years of wandering far from the pleasures of home, Molly's many lovers are the modern equivalent of the insolent suitors that gather round Penelope in Ulysses's palace.

Although Stephen (Telemachus) and Bloom (Ulysses) complement each other and are connected by a complex system of correspondences, parallels and symbols, it is their destiny to narrowly miss one another all day until they finally meet in 'Circe'.

What am I following him for? Bloom wonders as he follows Stephen into Nighttown. *Still*, he concludes, *he's the best of that lot*.[291] There is something about this wayward young man that arouses the father in Bloom and earlier he notes with almost paternal approval that Stephen is wearing a better pair of shoes than the last time he saw him (they are Mulligan's cast-offs).[292]

He finds Stephen in Bella Cohen's brothel. Surrounded by chattering prostitutes, Stephen plays the pianola and talks learnedly but drunkenly on the themes that have preoccupied him all day. In the visionary, hallucinatory atmosphere of this absinthe-fuelled episode, several of the people he has met reappear (including a mocking, clownish Mulligan) and his imagination runs riot. Similarly, in the presence of Bella, the *massive whoremistress*, Bloom's subconscious desires come to the fore and he indulges (in his imagination) in a sado-masochistic fantasy with her until Bella turns into a man (Bello) and Bloom is transformed into a quivering, submissive female.[293] Joyce gives full reign to Bloom's furtive lust and shaming desires, his fear that any outlet he might find for his sexual frustrations will get him into trouble with the authorities; a theme he would elaborate upon in *Finnegans Wake* with the sexual guilt of Humphrey Chimpden Earwicker. This is the phantasmagoric climax of Bloom's day and, as well as finally meeting Stephen, he also encounters the ghosts of his father and grandfather.

While dancing with the prostitutes, Stephen, too, is brought up short by a vision of his mother, *her face worn and noseless, green with grave mould.*[294] He cries out in horror and smashes a chandelier with his ashplant. Bella calls for the police and Stephen makes a hasty exit. Sensible Bloom picks up Stephen's ashplant and uses all of his tact and diplomacy to calm down Bella, leaving a shilling to cover the damage.

Outside Stephen drunkenly approaches a young woman while her two soldier escorts are relieving themselves elsewhere. The British soldiers, privates Carr and Compton, are spoiling for a fight when Bloom catches up with Stephen at the corner of Beaver Street. Stephen's remark that he *must kill the priest and the king* in his mind only inflames the situation.[295] Private Carr will not tolerate this slur on Edward VII: *He rushes towards Stephen, fists outstretched, and strikes him in the face. Stephen totters, collapses, falls stunned. He lies prone, his face to the sky, his hat rolling to the wall.*[296] Bloom fetches the hat and helps Stephen to his feet. Stephen is delirious, murmuring poetry, and Bloom's paternal solicitude conjures up a final vision: his dead son Rudy.

In the next episode, 'Eumaeus', Bloom takes Stephen to a cabman's shelter (fancifully run by Skin-the-Goat – James Fitzharris – an accessory to the Phoenix Park Murders) to sober him up and invites him home to 7 Eccles Street.

In Homer's *Odyssey*, when Ulysses is reunited with Telemachus it is a cause for great rejoicing. 'I am no more but thy father,' he says in Lamb's version. 'I am that Ulysses by reason of whose absence thy youth has been exposed to such wrongs from injurious men . . . I am he that after twenty years absence, and suffering a world of ill, have recovered at last the sight of my country earth.' In *Ulysses*, however, having reached this crucial plot-point, Joyce mischievously drains it of all dramatic potency. 'Eumaeus' is full of yawns, clichés and redundant clauses, because Stephen and Bloom are exhausted; while the next episode, 'Ithaca', is written *in the form of a mathematical catechism*, so that the reader will *know everything and know it in the baldest coldest way*.[297]

Bloom senses that he and Stephen have much in common: they are both sensitive to art and cosmopolitan in outlook, rejecting the insularity of Dublin, and both are prepared to question society's norms, nationalism and orthodox religions. Stephen, on the other hand, is rather condescending towards Bloom, though he finds him pleasant enough company for the time being. They don't see eye to eye on everything, either: Bloom loves water and washing (he visits a Turkish bath in 'Lotus Eaters'), while Stephen claims to be a *hydrophobe* (like Joyce) and hasn't had a bath since October (Bloom charitably attributes this lack of hygiene to his artistic temperament).[298] Also Bloom cannot entirely accept Stephen's belief in the *eternal affirmation of the spirit of man in literature*.[299]

Bloom is the perfect host and takes a *vicarious satisfaction* in Stephen, while Stephen, for the most part, maintains a brooding silence (Bloom assumes he is busy composing verses in his head).[300] The prospect of striking up a friendship with this young genius excites his imagination: Stephen is not his son, but he would make an excellent son-in-law. The high point comes when he offers Stephen a room for the night.

Was the proposal of asylum accepted? asks the narrator-examiner.

Promptly, inexplicably, with amicability, gratefully it was declined.[301]

The union of this modern-day Ulysses with his 'son' is a temporary one, with none of the fanfares of the Homeric original. Reluctant to say goodbye, Bloom suggests circumstances in which they might meet again: Stephen and Molly could give each other lessons in Italian and singing respectively and perhaps he and Bloom might meet from time to time for intellectual discussions. Stephen is polite but noncommittal.

Leaving the house, they gaze up at the stars, contemplating the immensity of the universe and the smallness of their own lives. They relieve themselves in the garden and then Bloom and Stephen bid each other goodnight. And yet something has passed between them. Before shaking hands they stand in silence, *each contemplating the other in both mirrors of the reciprocal flesh of theirhisnothis fellowfaces.*[302] Stephen and Bloom, *Stoom* and *Blephen*,[303] are one and the same: Stephen is the head and Bloom the heart, Stephen the mind and Bloom the body.

In Homer's story (as Lamb tells it), Ulysses's long journey back to Ithaca is 'crowned with the enjoyment of his virtuous and true wife Penelope'. In Joyce's reworking, Bloom climbs into bed beside Molly, lying with his head at her feet. She asks him where he has been and who he has been talking to downstairs. He tells her about Stephen, then tenderly kisses each of her buttocks before losing consciousness: *He rests. He has travelled.*[304]

Unimpressed by this gesture of reconciliation, Molly suspects he has been with a prostitute. Her monologue ('Penelope') is one of the most famous sections of *Ulysses*: *It turns like the huge earth ball*, said Joyce, *slowly surely and evenly round and round spinning, its four cardinal points being the female breasts, arse, womb and cunt expressed by the words* because, bottom *(in all senses bottom button, bottom of the class, bottom of the sea, bottom of his heart),* woman, yes.[305] Molly's consciousness really is a stream: her thoughts are unpunctuated and flow as rapidly as her bladder as she squats on the chamber pot. Joyce associated women with water and would make his next heroine, Anna Livia Plurabelle, the River Liffey itself.

As Molly contemplates the men in her life – her father, her husband and her lovers – Bloom's final battle is out of his hands. It is up to Penelope to clasp Ulysses to her again. But will she?

Molly is still savouring her energetic afternoon with 'Blazes' Boylan and even contemplates becoming *Mrs Boylan*.[306] He is richer than Bloom and she's tired of scrimping and saving all the time: *Here we are as bad as ever after 16 years.*[307] Why can't Bloom get a proper job in an office or a bank? He led her to believe he would amount to something when they were courting. But Boylan isn't serious about Molly and she didn't like the *determined vicious look in his eye* when they made love.[308] He might have been more virile than Bloom, but he was rough and thoughtless, leaving her unsatisfied. She senses his contempt for women, whereas Bloom understands *what a woman is*.[309]

Boylan, who *has no manners nor no refinement*, is briefly replaced in her fantasies by the *handsome young poet* Stephen: *what a pity he didnt stay . . . theres the room upstairs empty and Millys bed in the back room he could do his writing and studies at the table in there*.[310] She imagines serving him breakfast in bed wearing *a nice semitransparent morning gown* and looks forward to meeting him for 'lessons'.[311]

On the other hand Bloom has been a good husband *and looks after his wife and family*.[312] Molly is impressed by his general knowledge and feels protective of him when people make fun behind his back. *Ill just give him one more chance*, she thinks.[313] She'll get up early and serve him breakfast while wearing her *best shift and drawers let him have a good eyeful* and see what he's missing.[314] And then, in one of the most famous passages in modern literature, she recalls lying with him in the rhododendrons on Howth Hill (on the north-east coast of Dublin Bay) on the day she first gave herself to him: *he asked me to say yes and I wouldnt answer first only looked out over the sea and the sky . . . and I thought well as well him as another and then I asked him with my eyes to ask again yes and then he asked me would I yes to say yes my mountain flower and first I put my arms around him yes and drew him down to me so he could feel my breasts all perfume yes and his heart was going like mad and yes I said yes I will Yes.*[315]

Joyce regarded *Yes* as *the most positive word in the human language* and Molly's final promiscuous *Yes* to life signals Bloom's victory.[316]

O! Infamy!

The pity is, said Joyce, *the public will demand and find a moral in my book, or worse they may take it in some serious way, and on the honour of a gentleman, there is not one single serious line in it.*[317] This did not prevent Ezra Pound from reading *Ulysses* as a satire on modern society. 'The sticky, molasses-covered filth of current print, all the fuggs, all the foetors, the whole boil of the European mind has been lanced,' he announced.[318] For Pound the twentieth century was 'without dignity, without tragedy', but Joyce's vision is broader and more humane than this.[319] In keeping with the artistic programme he outlined in 'Drama and Life', *Ulysses* is about the *great human comedy in which each has share.*[320]

Pound praised *Ulysses* as a 'super-novel . . . an epoch-making report on the state of the human mind in the twentieth century'.[321] Yeats thought Joyce had 'surpassed in intensity any novelist of our time', though he later admitted to not having finished *Ulysses*.[322] For T S Eliot it was 'the most important expression which the modern age has found; it is a book to which we are all indebted but from which none of us can

Infamous: Joyce in 1923

escape.'[323] Virginia Woolf was unimpressed by 'the first 200 pages of *Ulysses*. Never did I read such tosh. As for the first 2 chapters we will let them pass, but the 3rd 4th 5th 6th – merely the scratching of pimples on the body of the bootboy at Claridges. Of course genius may blaze out on page 652 but I have my doubts. And this is what Eliot worships.'[324] Nevertheless, *Ulysses* is regarded as a major influence on her novel *Mrs Dalloway* (1925).

'*Ulysses* was and remains the first great masterpiece of anti-heroic literature; if the novel has survived it, there is yet an uneasy feeling abroad that it has not recovered from the shock.'
Anthony Cronin[325]

The critic Shane Leslie, reviewing *Ulysses* in the *Quarterly Review*, found it 'unreadable, unquotable, and unreviewable', thereby alerting the Home Office to a possible case for censorship. A secret Home Office report advised that 'if it [*Ulysses*] is ever found open in the post it should be detained.'[326] Leslie went on to compare *Ulysses* to the famous Fenian bombing of Clerkenwell prison. It is 'an attempted Clerkenwell explosion in the well-guarded, well-built, classical prison of English Literature. The bomb has exploded . . . All that is unmentionable, according to civilised standards, has been brought to the light of day without any veil of decency.'[327]

'I rather wish I had never read [*Ulysses*]. It gives me an inferiority complex. When I read a book like that and then come back to my own work, I feel like a eunuch who has taken a course in voice production and can pass himself off fairly well as a bass or a baritone, but if you listen closely you can hear the good old squeak just the same as ever.'
George Orwell[328]

Joyce delayed another trip to Dublin, but Nora wanted to see her mother. On 1 April 1922, shortly after the publication of *Ulysses* and against Joyce's wishes, she took Giorgio and Lucia to Dublin. They visited John Joyce and the following day travelled to Galway. Back in Paris Joyce was at his wit's end. Not only had Nora threatened never to return, but Ireland was in a state of civil war. In January the Dáil

Giorgio, Nora and Lucia, Galway 1922

had ratified the Anglo-Irish Treaty and the country had divided into two camps: pro-Treaty and anti-Treaty, Free State troops and the Irish Republican Army (IRA).

In Galway, Free State soldiers marched into Nora's bedroom to train their guns on a warehouse across the road occupied by the IRA. When Joyce heard of this he immediately arranged for a plane to pick them up, but Nora and the children had already fled. As Joyce tells it: *They ran through the town to the station and escaped in a train lying flat on their bellies (the two females that is) amid a fusillade which continued for an hour from right and left between troops on the train and ambushes along the line.*[329] Nora, Giorgio and Lucia got back to Paris unharmed, but Joyce took this attack on his family personally.

At a party the following month he was introduced to the great French novelist Marcel Proust, author of *In Search of Lost Time* (1912–22). They had little in common and had not read each other's work, so the meeting was not a success. However, one thing is certain: Joyce envied Proust his cork-lined bedroom at 102 Boulevard Haussmann where he wrote his multi-volume masterpiece cut off from the outside world. To Joyce's immense credit, he wrote all of his books with *people coming in and out* and was besieged by domestic distractions.[330] He wrote as he lived, immersed in the chaos of the real world, not hidden away in some ivory tower.

In August, recovering from another bout of iritis, he travelled to London to meet Miss Weaver for the first time. She looked forward to his next book, which he told her would be *a history of the world*.[331] But whether he would write another book depended more than ever on the state of his eyes. They were red all of the time and the London ophthalmologists he consulted diagnosed the onset of glaucoma. After a brief pause in Paris, he travelled with Nora to Nice where a doctor applied leeches to his eyes and it was here that his new book began to take shape in his mind.

Joyce in the
South of
France 1922

On 12 December 1922 the first copy of *Ulysses* was confiscated at Croydon Airport, London, by a Customs official. He no doubt bore some resemblance to the Customs officer in Evelyn Waugh's *Vile Bodies* (1930), who considers the manuscript of Adam Fenwick-Symes's autobiography (written in Paris) to be 'downright dirt, and we burns that straight away, see . . . I knows dirt when I sees it . . . Particularly against books the Home Secretary is. If we can't stamp out literature in the country, we can at least stop its being brought in from outside.'[332]

Customs and Excise pressed the Home Office for an early decision as to whether *Ulysses* should be prohibited as indecent or returned to its owner. 'The importer describes it as a noteworthy work of art by an author of considerable repute which is being seriously discussed in the highest literary circles,' said the Customs report.[333] A week later Sir Archibald Bodkin, the Director of Public Prosecutions, made his judgement: 'As might be supposed, I have not had the time nor the inclination to read through this book. I have, however, read pages 690 to 732.'[334] He had somehow alighted on 'Penelope', which Joyce admitted was *probably more obscene than any preceding episode.*[335]

'I am entirely unable to appreciate how those pages are relevant to the rest of the book,' Sir Archibald complained, 'or indeed what the book itself is about. I can discover no story. There is no introduction which gives a key to its purpose and the pages above mentioned, written as they are, as if composed by a more or less illiterate vulgar woman, form an entirely detached part of this production.' It also contained 'a great deal of unmitigated filth and obscenity . . . The book appears to have been printed as a limited edition in Paris, where I notice the author, perhaps prudently, resides . . . In my opinion the book is obscene and indecent, and on that ground the Customs authorities would be justified in refusing to part with it. It is conceivable that there will be criticism of this attitude towards a well-known writer; the answer will be that filthy books are not allowed to be imported into this country.'[336]

Customs and Excise, the Post Office and the police were ordered to seize all copies of *Ulysses* entering Britain and discreet enquiries were made among booksellers as to anyone who might have ordered a copy. In January 1923 a senior Home Office official wrote that any journals or newspapers that had reviewed *Ulysses* had 'done a disservice both to English literature and to public decency . . . The fear is that other writers with a love of notoriety will attempt to write in the same vein.'[337] Three months later, 500 copies of *Ulysses* were seized at Folkestone and destroyed.

In July 1926 the Home Office discovered that 'a dangerous crank' – in fact the literary critic F R Leavis (1895–1978) – had asked a Cambridge bookseller for a copy of *Ulysses* and was proposing to lecture on it.[338] Sir Archibald wrote to the Vice Chancellor of Cambridge University, reminding him of the ban and threatening to prosecute any student found with a copy. 'It was hardly to be credited that this book should be proposed as the subject of lectures in any circumstances but above all that it should be the subject of discussion and be available for the use of a mixed body of students,' he said. 'I do not pretend to be a critic of what is, I suppose, literature . . . but there are many passages in it which are indecent and entirely unsuitable to bring to the attention of any person of either sex.'[339] He requested the Chief Constable of Cambridge to let him know if Leavis so much as mentioned *Ulysses* in his lectures. The lectures were cancelled.

The Strangest Dream that was ever Halfdreamt

In *Ulysses* Joyce professed to be more interested in the conscious than the unconscious mind, but this emphasis shifted dramatically when he came to write his next book. Dreams have their own rules, unbounded by the laws of the waking world, and his new work would be an attempt to represent the mind asleep: *One great part of every human existence is passed in a state which cannot be rendered sensible by the use of wideawake language, cutandry grammar and goahead plot.*[340] But what would the unconscious sound like? It wouldn't necessarily speak in English or any other language. It would more likely be a babble of all the languages known to man. But neither would it be perfectly coherent, for the unconscious is chaotic and unpredictable and it is up to the subconscious mind to organize our thoughts and impulses. Joyce would have to invent a new language that somehow replicated the slips and sudden glitches, the dislocations and discontinuities of dreams.

This hugely ambitious project needs to be placed in context. Joyce was now famous: his name was mentioned in the same breath as the psychoanalyst Sigmund Freud (1856–1939) and the physicist Albert Einstein (1879–1955), whose ground-breaking theories had so captured the public imagination. *Ulysses* was hailed as a psychological as much as a literary breakthrough and for T S Eliot it had 'the importance of a scientific discovery. No one else has built a novel upon such a foundation before . . . In using the myth, in manipulating a continuous parallel between contemporaneity and antiquity, Mr Joyce is pursuing a method which others must pursue after him. They will not be imitators, any more than the scientist who uses the discoveries of Einstein in pursuing his own, independent, further investigations. It is simply a way of controlling, of ordering, of giving a shape and a significance to the immense panorama of futility and anarchy which is contemporary history.'[341] The notion that Joyce was the equal of Freud or Einstein emerged, in part, from the aims and ambitions of Modernism, but he quietly accepted this assessment of his role. His *imitation of the dream-state* baffled and irritated many of his admirers, but it made perfect sense for Joyce the literary scientist to set himself such a forbidding challenge.[342] This is why he persevered with his new book against the wishes of his supporters and this is why it has no equal in literature.

Joyce drew freely on the collective unconscious – myths and legends, historical events, monumental conflicts between gods or races – but he also realized that in order to retain an element of characterization in the flux of the unconscious he would have to create archetypal characters. By 1923 he had found a name for this strange experiment: *Finnegans Wake*, meaning both *the wake and the awakening of Finn*, the legendary giant Finn MacCool and, by extension, the awakening of the Irish people and all the oppressed Finnegans of the world.[343] Finn is sleeping only until the hour that Ireland needs him (much as it was said that Parnell was not dead, but waiting to be called in Ireland's time of need). The title of Joyce's new book remained a secret, however, and it was known only as his *Work in Progress*.

The collective unconscious was the psychoanalyst Carl Jung's term for that part of the unconscious which is shared by everyone, the residue of common cultural experiences. In the collective unconscious certain ideas and images become archetypes (primitive mental images inherited from man's earliest ancestors). Joyce knew of Jung's ideas, but struck out on his own and refused to admit their influence on him.

It was Stanislaus's party piece as a child to sing 'Finnegan's Wake', an Irish-American vaudeville ballad. Tim Finnegan, a drunken hod-carrier, falls from a ladder, breaking his skull. At his wake a fight breaks out and 'a noggin of whiskey' is thrown on the bed where Finnegan rests in peace. The whiskey revives him and he cries out 'Whirl your liquor round like blazes . . . do ye think I'm dead?' From this simple story Joyce was to create a potent meditation on the Fall of man and the Resurrection and to celebrate the ability of frail, culpable, mortal humanity to be reborn again and again (*Hohohoho, Mister Finn, you're going to be Mister Finnagain!*).[344]

Tim Finnegan lived in Walkin Street,
  A gentleman Irish mighty odd.
He had a tongue both rich and sweet,
  An' to rise in the world he carried a hod.

Now Tim had a sort of a tipplin' way,
  With the love of the liquor he was born,
An' to help him on his way to work each day,
  He'd a drop of the craythur every morn.

from the ballad 'Finnegan's Wake'

The first thing Joyce wrote after *Ulysses* was a sketch of King Roderick O'Conor, *the paramount chief polemarch and last pre-electric king of Ireland.*[345] On 10 March 1923 he found a pen and wrote two pages in large letters so that he could read them. He was groping his way towards a new style and tone, jaunty, tongue-in-cheek, light-hearted, weird, the language complex and many-layered.

In the summer Joyce and his family stayed at a boarding house in Bognor, England. It was here that he came up with the word *quark* to imitate the squawking seagulls and the first section of *Work in Progress* to be published (in the *transatlantic review* in April 1924) begins *Three quarks for Muster Mark!* [346] Over the next 15 years fragments of *Work in Progress* would appear in the avant-garde literary journal *transition*, including one of the most beautiful and accessible sections of the book, 'Anna Livia Plurabelle'. Joyce described it as *a chattering dialogue* across Dublin's River Liffey *by two washerwomen who as night falls become a tree and a stone. The river is named Anna Liffey*, and because Dublin was founded by Vikings *some of the words at the beginning are hybrid Danish-*

English.[347] It incorporates the names of 350 rivers and took him at least 1,200 hours to write.

Joyce loved the idea of entering uncharted territory. *Every novelist knows the recipe*, he told a friend. *It is not very difficult to follow a simple, chronological scheme which the critics will understand.* But he was determined to tell his story *in a new way . . . I am trying to build many planes of narrative with a single esthetic purpose.*[348] To another friend he grandly announced *Je suis au bout de l'anglais* ('I've come to the end of English').[349] As long ago as 1907 he had threatened to unlearn English and write in French or Italian. He didn't, because he loved the English language, but while writing *Ulysses* he realized that even English had its limitations. *I'd like a language which is above all languages*, he said. *I cannot express myself in English without enclosing myself in a tradition.*[350] He had come a long way from the young man who had once hated the Austro-Hungarian Empire *with its hundred races and thousand languages.*[351] Now he celebrated multilingualism, using at least 40 languages in *Finnegans Wake*. Joyce was an incorrigible punster and in his new work he elevated the pun to the level of a serious literary device that allowed him to conflate several languages at once.

Joyce was not alone in wanting to explode the logic of words. It was one of the main aims of Dadaism and then Surrealism. Contemporaries such as Gertrude Stein (1874–1946), August Stramm (1874–1915), Léon-Paul Fargue (1876–1947), Hans Arp (1887–1966), Antonin Artaud (1896–1948) and Michel Leiris (1901–90) also sought to liberate words from their accustomed connections.

His new book, he insisted, was *pure music*, written more for the ear than the eye.[352] *If anyone doesn't understand a passage*, he said, *all he need do is read it aloud.*[353] Sound takes precedence over meaning, making *soundsense and sensesound kin again . . . Can you not distinguish the sense, prain, from the sound, bray?*[354] Joyce often horrified his translators by caring more for the sound of words than their meaning, and in many respects the translations he oversaw are entirely new creations.

His fame assured with *Ulysses*, Joyce amused himself by including numerous references to his private life in his new book, some of which not even his closest friends could have known. *Finnegans Wake* is, in short, a kind of autobiography: self-contained, solipsistic, indulgent, even a little egotistical. *I don't care if the whole thing crumbles when I have done with it*, he said, but of course he did.[355] Towards the end of his life the *Wake* meant a great deal more to him than *Ulysses*, which he tended to disparage.

Finnegans Wake is impossible to summarize. No single narrative thread takes precedence, but all exist simultaneously. *There are in a way no characters*, said Joyce. *It's like a dream. The style is also changing, and unrealistic, like the dream world.*[356] In fact, the central problem of the *Wake* is that much of it might mean anything – *So you need hardly spell me how every word will be bound over to carry three score and ten toptypsical readings.*[357]

On one level *Finnegans Wake* is 'about' Mr Porter, who runs a public house in Chapelizod, and what goes on *in the licensed boosiness primises of his delhightful bazar.*[358] Chapelizod (Chapel of Iseult or Isolde) is west of Dublin and in the 1870s Joyce's father worked at the Chapelizod distillery on the Liffey. His stories about a man called Broadbent who owned the Mullingar Hotel in Chapelizod probably inspired Joyce's innkeeper hero. Mr Porter's public house might be *the Mullingar Inn*, although the *Wake* mentions several pubs both real and imaginary.[359] It has even been suggested that Mr Porter's inn is *Dublinn*.[360]

So, at the level closest to reality, we are in the sleeping mind of a middle-aged publican called Mr Porter (*missed a porter*).[361] He and his wife are asleep in their bedroom above the pub. *The Porters*, we are told, *are very nice people.* Mr Porter is *an excellent forefather* and his wife *a most kindhearted messmother.*[362] They have three *little Porter babes*: twins Kevin and Jerry, and a daughter, Isobel.[363]

It is, in short, a *united family pateramater*, but it isn't perfect.[364] Mr Porter's wife no longer attracts him and he is prey to *incestuous temptations* towards Isobel.[365] In the last chapter of Book III he and his wife 'awaken' (but not really, it is still part of his dream) and unsuccessfully attempt intercourse.

So far so good, but at the level of the collective unconscious Mr Porter and his family are transformed into archetypes. He becomes Humphrey Chimpden Earwicker, the true hero of the *Wake*, whose initials are woven throughout the text: *Here Comes Everybody*, *Haveth Childers Everywhere*, *He'll Cheat E'erawan*, *Howth Castle and Environs* and even H_2CE_3.[366] He is all the men who have ever lived, are living, and have yet to be born. He is Everyman or even Ireland itself (*Eireweeker*).[367] There are also elements of Joyce and his father in Earwicker, with his *blueygreen eyes a bit scummy developing a series of angry boils with certain references to the Deity, seeking relief in alcohol and so on*.[368]

Earwicker goes through numerous incarnations. For instance, 'Earwicker' reminds Joyce of 'earwig', the French for which is *perce-oreille*, so Earwicker becomes Persse O'Reilly. Everyone in the *Wake* suffers from a similar chain of adventitious associations that mutate them into somebody else. When Earwicker is the biblical Noah, he is also Sir Noah Guinness, the Dublin brewer (*Ghinees hies good for you*).[369] If he is Isaac, son of Abraham, he is also Isaac Butt, Parnell's predecessor, or Isaac Bickerstaff, a pseudonym of Jonathan Swift. And so on.

The slumbering Mrs Porter, exhausted after a busy Saturday evening in the bar, is transformed in the collective unconscious into Earwicker's red-headed wife, Anna Livia Plurabelle, an archetypal woman and therefore Everywoman. Whereas Earwicker's symbol is a phallic mountain, hers is a river: she is the River Liffey and her life comes to an end as it flows out into the sea.

In the logic of Mr Porter's dream his sleeping son Kevin becomes Shaun the Post (a purloiner of other people's mail). He is either a type of cynical politician (*I heard a voice, the voce of Shaun, vote of the Irish*) or a sanctimonious priest and represents the moral hypocrisy of bourgeois society.[370] There is something of Joyce's more sensible brother Stanislaus (*Stainusless*) about Shaun, who also goes by the names of Jaunty Jaun, Haun, Yawn and many others.[371] Outwardly more successful than his twin brother, he is secretly jealous of him.

Their other son, Jerry, becomes Shem the penman, and it is a short step from Shem to Seumas to James. Shem is an artist, but also a coward and fond of a drop or two. He is also Hosty the balladeer, composer of the scurrilous 'Ballad of Persse O'Reilly', so he is not the most supportive son.

Shem is a wry self-caricature and Joyce does not spare himself as an object of ridicule. He laughs at his Stephen Dedalus years, claiming that no one *ever nursed such a spoiled opinion of his monstrous marvellosity as did this mental and moral defective* who can't hold his drink and is *always blaspheming, so holy writ* and going on and on about *Shakhisheard*.[372] Like Stephen, Shem *will neither serve not let serve, pray nor let pray*, nor is he prepared to suffocate in Ireland: *he would not throw himself in Liffey . . . he refused to saffrocake himself with a sod*.[373] He was for some time *absinthe-minded, with his Paris address!* and worked in a Berlitz School (*beurlads scoel*) before settling down to write *a (suppressed) book*, followed by his *word in pregross*.[374] Shem is *an Irish emigrant the wrong way out*, a truly international *Europasianised Afferyank*.[375] During the First World War and at the time of the Easter Rising, *a rank funk getting the better of him*, he *kuskykorked himself up tight in his inkbattle house, badly the worse for boosegas*.[376]

Shem and Shaun are characters from nineteenth-century theatre. The stage Irishman Sean the Post appears in Dion Boucicault's *Arrah-na-Pogue*. Shem is a stage villain (and a forger like Pigott) in Sir Charles Young's *Jim the Penman*. Joyce also remembered two feeble-minded brothers in Dublin who were nicknamed Shem and Shaun.

Shem and Shaun complement each other, being in fact two sides of their father's personality (it's his dream, after all). If Earwicker is Adam, Shaun is Abel to Shem's Cain. When Shaun is the Archangel Michael (Mick), Shem is Lucifer (Old Nick). Shem and Shaun have other incarnations: Dolph and Kevin, Taff and Butt, the Gripes and the Mookse, Hengest and Horsa, Mutt and Jute, the Gracehoper and the Ondt (a retelling of La Fontaine's 'Fable of the Grasshopper and the Ant'), the actors Mr Seumas McQuillad and Mr Sean O'Mailey (who play Glugg and Chuff in 'The Mime of Mick, Nick and the Maggies') and Caddy (or the Cad) and Primas: *Primas was a santryman and drilled all decent people. Caddy went to Winehouse and wrote a peace a farce. Blotty words for Dublin.*[377]

As they are both aspects of their father, the twins also take it in turns to be Parnell. When Shem is Parnell, Shaun is his betrayer, the politician Tim Healy, but when Shaun is Parnell, Shem the penman is the forger Richard Pigott. Sometimes the twins gain a third personality. When Earwicker is Noah, for instance, Shem and Shaun are his three sons: Shem, Ham and Japhet (or *shame, humbug and profit*), just as Caseous (Cassius) and Burrus (Brutus) gain Antonius (Antony).[378] Similarly, three soldiers witness Earwicker's ambiguous crime with the two girls in Phoenix Park. Who is the third soldier? It has been suggested he

The tragedy of Tristan and Isolde originated in ancient Celtic legend. Tristan, a medieval knight, defeats the giant Morold, but suffers a serious wound, which is healed by Isolde, the daughter of the queen of Ireland. To cement an alliance between Ireland and Cornwall, Tristan takes the Irish princess to Cornwall to marry his uncle, King Mark. On the journey, Isolde and Tristan accidentally drink a love potion and fall madly in love. One of Mark's knights realizes this and mortally wounds Tristan, who dies in Isolde's arms.

is Earwicker himself – he is his own worst enemy.

Just as their mother is a river and their father a mountain,

Shaun is a tree and Shem a stone. And so this tale told of Shaun and Shem becomes a tale of *stem or stone*; as night falls they become indistinguishable and unite as *tree-stone* or *Treestone* and eventually *Tristan*, in love with Isolde (*Trustan with Usolde*).[379]

But if there are two Tristans, there must be two Isoldes. In his dream, Mr Porter's 16-year-old daughter Isobel becomes Earwicker's daughter, Issy. There is only one of her to represent Everygirl, so she has a split personality: virgin and whore, innocent and sexual predator. (Her schizoid character also represents the rivalry between Esther and Stella, two women in Jonathan Swift's life.) Issy is the two Mary Magdalens (the Maggies in the 'Mime') and also Izod/Isolde/ Iseult, *a bewitching blonde who dimples delightfully*.[380] She is sometimes the Blessed Virgin, sometimes an idealized girl (*Nuvoletta in her lightdress*), but she is also a *Pair of Sloppy Sluts* in Phoenix Park.[381] When Earwicker is Parnell, Issy is Kitty O'Shea. In fact, she is all of Earwicker's temptresses, including two strapping barmaids (or *two stripping baremaids*).[382] When Issy seduces Earwicker, she also seduces his alter egos, Shem and Shaun, to whom she is something more than their *fond sister Izzy* (in fact, she is two *saucicissters*).[383] She writes amorous letters to Shaun (*you, sis,* he says, *that used to write to us the exceeding nice letters*), but she is more attracted to the reprobate artist Shem: *Coach me how to tumble, Jaime* [Shem/James/*j'aime* ('I love')], *and listen, with supreme regards, Juan* [Shaun/Don Juan], *in haste, warn me which to ah ah ah ah . . .* [384]

In his *Journal to Stella* (1710–13) Jonathan Swift (1667–1745) uses a kind of baby-talk that can be heard in the language of *Finnegans Wake*. Stella (Esther Johnson) had a rival in Esther Vanhomrigh, who entered Swift's life in 1708 and was intensely jealous of Stella.

Rivals in love as in everything else, Shem and Shaun are always fighting each other in various guises. Occasionally they are reconciled and unite to overthrow their father, but this show of unity does not last because history repeats itself. War and peace are cyclical: *So that when we shall have acquired unification we shall pass on to diversity and when we shall have passed on to diversity we shall have acquired the instinct of combat and when we shall have acquired the instinct of combat we shall pass back to the spirit of appeasement.*[385] Sometimes Shem wins, sometimes Shaun and sometimes they swap characters. As their mother says, *they've changed their characticuls – Them boys is so contrary.*[386] But if Shem and Shaun are always making war – then peace, then war again – it is Anna Livia who reconciles victor and vanquished. *Annah the Allmaziful, the Everliving, the Bringer of Plurabilities* also brings harmony and reconciliation.[387] But like Helen of Troy, men fight over her. She starts the *penisolate war* and the cycle begins all over again.[388]

He might be a hero, but Earwicker also commits the central crime of the book and spends much of his time being hounded by his enemies (like Parnell or Oscar Wilde). He is a sinner par excellence, accused *of having behaved with ongentilmensky immodus opposite a pair of dainty maidservants* near the Wellington monument in Phoenix Park.[389] Joyce is alluding to the Phoenix Park Murders, but also to a more personal event: *The encounter between my father and a tramp (the basis of my book) actually took place at that part of the park.*[390] John Joyce was attacked and had to defend his rate-collector's pouch.

Earwicker's crime is the Original Sin of the *Wake*, but the exact nature of his *alleged misdemeanour* is unclear.[391] Did he spy on two micturating girls or expose himself to them or proposition them or just masturbate while thinking about them? They are young enough to be his daughter and Earwicker's crime is intimately associated with his feelings for Issy.

Having repressed his incestuous desires, *Haromphrey* suffers from a stammer that gives him away: *our mewmew mutual daughters . . . I am woo-woo willing.*[392] It occurs most of all when he is trying to defend himself, as when *a cad with a pipe* asks him the time in Phoenix Park and he takes this opportunity to clear his name: *there is not one tittle of truth, allow me to tell you, in that purest of fibfib fabrications . . .*[393] Confronted by the pipe-smoking Cad (Caddy/ Shem), Earwicker knows that *Hesitency was clearly to be evitated,* but he can't help himself.[394] *Hesitency* is a crucial word in the *Wake*, indicating not only Earwicker's guilt (*HeCitEncy!*) about his illicit feelings (*hiscitendency*), but also the spelling mistake in Richard Pigott's forged letter incriminating Parnell.[395]

Forgery is a major theme. Shaun complains of Shem's writing that *Every dimmed letter in it is a copy* and Joyce seems to admit as much: *what do you think Vulgariano* [Shem/Joyce] *did but study with stolen fruit how cutely to copy all their various styles of signature so as one day to utter an epical forged cheque on the public for his own priovate profit.*[397] He seems to be saying that all writing – all literature – is a kind of forgery and *Finnegans Wake* is *The last word in stolen-telling!*[398] Joyce stole from all over the place, even his own books, from the opening sentence of *A Portrait* (*Eins within a space and a wearywide space it wast ere wohned a Mookse*) to *Ulysses*, his *usylessly unreadable Blue Book of Eccles* (referring to its blue cover and Bloom's Eccles Street address).[399] For instance, the line *Good morning, have you used Pears' soap* in *Ulysses* becomes *Guld modning, have yous viewsed Piers' aube?* in the *Wake*; just as *Ess Ess. O ess* in the *Wake* echoes Molly's final *Yes* in *Ulysses* (as well as an SOS signal).[400]

Oliver Gogarty called *Finnegans Wake* 'the most colossal leg pull in literature since Macpherson's *Ossian*'.[396] The third-century Gaelic bard Ossian's 'rediscovered' poems were the literary sensation of the 1760s, until it was revealed they had been forged by James Macpherson (1736–96).

Anna Livia intends to set the record straight about her husband's alleged misdemeanour, defending him in public though berating him in private. She will wash him clean, like the two washerwomen scrubbing clothes in the Liffey. The Earwickers are washing their dirty linen in public and the *Wake* 'ends' with the laundry, after *several rinsings . . . Clean*.[401]

Earwicker's public fall from grace is just one of many falls in the *Wake*, the most obvious being Tim Finnegan's fall from a ladder: *(There was a wall of course in erection) Dimb! He stottered from the latter Damb! he was dud*.[402] All erections must fall, of course, and impotence is another of Earwicker's (and Mr Porter's) problems *(Phall if you but will, rise you must)*.[403] There are also references to the Fall of Adam and Eve, the Wall Street Crash of 1929 and Humpty Dumpty's fall from a wall. Nevertheless, Earwicker (and, by extension, all mankind) remains *great in all things, in guilt and in glory*.[404] We are all *human, erring and condonable*.[405] As Stephen realizes in *A Portrait*, the important thing is *To live, to err, to fall, to triumph, to recreate life out of life!*[406]

History . . . is a nightmare from which I am trying to awake, said Stephen in *Ulysses*.[407] In *Finnegans Wake* history is a dream and the dreamer never awakens. Time is not chronological, but cyclical: *eggburst, eggblend, eggburial and hatch-as-hatch can*.[408] As Joyce said, *in my imitation of the dream-state, I effect in a few minutes what may have taken centuries to bring about*.[409] Having got no further than the first sentence of Karl Marx's *Das Kapital* (1867), Joyce preferred to arrive at his own view of history, borrowing whatever took his fancy from some rather obscure sources, in particular the Italian philosophers Giambattista Vico (1668–1744) and Giordano Bruno (*c*.1548–1600).

In his *Scienza Nuova* (1725–44) Vico divides human history into four recurring cycles: theocratic (divine), aristocratic (heroic), democratic (civil) and a transitional phase (generation). In the *Wake* each cycle is announced by a thunderbolt.[410] The mythical Irish giant Finn MacCool represents Vico's heroic era, whereas his modern-day counterparts – Earwicker and Tim Finnegan – are products of democracy. At the end of a cycle everything returns and starts again, *by a commodious vicus of recirculation* – and Joyce's book is cyclical too: *It ends in the middle of a sentence and begins in the middle of the same sentence.*[411]

Joyce first encountered Giordano Bruno while studying Italian. In *A Portrait*, Stephen's tutor says Bruno is *a terrible heretic*, to which Stephen replies that he was also *terribly burned* (Bruno's doctrine of universal love got him burned at the stake by the Inquisition).[412] Bruno believed that nothing in the universe is lost and everything is in a state of transformation. In the *Wake* Joyce borrows this idea as well as Bruno's theory of the synthesis of opposites: after a period of conflict there is a reconciliation, just as the warring brothers Shem and Shaun unite to overthrow their father. These, then, are the main themes of *Finnegans Wake*: the synthesis of opposites, the cyclical evolution of history and the overthrow of the father figure, be it Earwicker, God or the British.

In the *Wake* Ireland represents all nations, with Dublin as the universal city. Ireland's history mirrors the history of the world: a disunited land, constantly invaded and on the defensive. Every attack on the Irish is included, from the Battle of Clontarf (1014), in which the Irish defeated the Danes, to the ruthless campaigns of Oliver Cromwell (1599–1658) and William III (1650–1702). There are also references to the Easter Rising and the creation of the Irish Free State.

The *Wake* is catholic only in the sense of being all-embracing or universal, for it is most critical of orthodox religions, priests and holy wars. Joyce considered the Catholic Church to be the very opposite of spiritual, because it involved itself in trade and war and condoned imperialism, but all the major religions are mocked in the *Wake* – it is a comic *pantheomime*.[413] God is referred to as the *Dodgfather* or the *Cloudy father! Unsure! Nongood!*, *the Great Sommboddy within the Omniboss*.[414] There are scrambled versions of the Lord's Prayer (*Haar Faagher, wild heart in Homelan; harrod's be the naun*) and the Ten Commandments: *First thou shalt not smile. Twice thou shalt not love. Lust, thou shalt not commix idolatry.*[415] The Paternoster becomes the *farternoiser*, *mea culpa* ('by my fault') becomes *may he colp her*, the Holy Ghost is the *holocaust* and there are dozens of puns on St Augustine's cry of 'O felix culpa!' (the fortunate fall of Adam and Eve that gave us the chance to achieve grace), as well as parodies of the Last Supper, the Mass and the Eucharist.[417] The *Wake* is an attack on all established institutions, from the Church to the British Empire, and, of course, the English language, for it is Shem's declared ambition to *wipe alley english spooker, multaphoniaksically spuking, off the face of the erse.*[418]

'Joyce maims words. Why? Because meanings have been dulled, then lost, then perverted by their connotations (which have grown over them) until their effect on the mind is no longer what it was when they were fresh.'
William Carlos Williams[416]

Finnegans Wake is the fullest development of Joyce's pitch for immortality. He wrote it, he said, *to keep the critics busy for three hundred years.*[419] He did not relish the prospect of being remembered for Bloom alone and saw to it that *Finnegans Wake*, his irreverent anti-Bible, would require the same kind of exegetical labour as an ancient holy text, *sentenced to be nuzzled over a full trillion times for ever and a night till his noddle sink or swim by that ideal reader suffering from an ideal insomnia.*[420]

Some readers have never forgiven Joyce for being so cryptic. A good example is the phrase *fairescapading in his natsirt.*[421] Even if we have worked out that *natsirt* backwards is *tristan*, the reference depends on our knowing that Parnell is said to have fled down a fire escape in his nightshirt when about to be discovered with Kitty O'Shea. Similarly, how are we to know that *coffin acid odarkery* is a reference to Kevin Izod O'Doherty, a little-known nineteenth-century author?[422] Or that *larrons o'toolers clittering up and tombles a'buckets clottering down* refers to

Lawrence O'Toole, a Dublin bishop, and St Thomas à Becket?[423] Or that *Clontarf one love one fear* is the date of the Battle of Clontarf (1014), but also the telephone number of a public house in Chapelizod?[424]

I am only an Irish clown, said Joyce, *a great joker at the universe.*[425] When asked if there were many levels of meaning to be discovered in the *Wake* he said *No, no, it's meant to make you laugh.*[426] Even if people did not wholly understand his book, he hoped they would appreciate its humour: *perhaps the raving madness I write will survive*, he said, *and perhaps it is very funny.*[427] It is a far cry from Stephen Dedalus's youthful mission to forge in the smithy of his soul the uncreated conscience of his race, but Joyce had not lowered his sights. Now he was forging the uncreated unconscious of all the races of the world and sharing in the laughter of the gods.

'Joyce's incomprehensible novel, which has provided a living for generations of English Literature professors, represents a lamentable tendency in twentieth-century fiction: the quest for total obscurity. *Finnegans Wake* is the best example of modernism disappearing up its own fundament.'

J G Ballard[428]

Reading *Finnegans Wake* can be a frustrating experience – why can't Joyce tell his tale in *pure undefallen engelsk?*[429] No interpretation can be too literal and the reader is in danger of overdosing on interpretations rather than enjoying the music. Nevertheless, it deserves to be admired by anyone who takes the time and the trouble to get to know its peculiar dreamlike world. However, there is much that we still don't understand about the book – and Joyce no doubt threw in a few insoluble mysteries. Perhaps, in the end, as one commentator put it, '*Finnegans Wake* is about *Finnegans Wake*.'[430]

Inkbattle

It has been suggested that after *Ulysses* Joyce had nothing more to say, but if this is the case it took him 17 years of hard work and all of his mental rigour and strength to say it. The strain of writing *Finnegans Wake* left him *literally doubled in two from fatigue and cramp* and by May 1927 he seriously contemplated handing it over to somebody else (the Dublin-born poet James Stephens), but nothing came of the plan.[431] *Of course*, Joyce confided to Miss Weaver, *he would never take a fraction of the time or pains I take but so much the better for him and me and possibly for the book itself. If he consented to maintain three or four points which I consider essential and I showed him the threads he could finish the design . . . It would be a great load off my mind.*[432]

> 'Experiment? God forbid! Look at the results of experiment in the case of a writer like Joyce. He started off writing very well, then you can watch his going mad with vanity. He ends up a lunatic.'
> Evelyn Waugh in the *Paris Review*, 1962

Stanislaus thought *Work in Progress* was an elaborate practical joke. 'You have done the longest day in literature,' he complained, 'and now you are conjuring up the deepest night.'[433] Pound could 'make nothing of it whatever . . . nothing short of divine vision or a new cure for the clapp can possibly be worth all the circumambient peripherization. Doubtless there are patient souls, who will wade through anything for the sake of the possible joke.'[434] Miss Weaver thought Pound had a point. 'I do not care much for . . . the darknesses and unintelligibilities of your deliberately-entangled language system,' she told Joyce. 'It seems to me you are wasting your genius.'[435]

The poor reception of *Work in Progress* strained Joyce's nerves and damaged his health. He lost weight worrying about it. *I am more and more aware of the indignant hostility shown to my experiment in interpreting the 'dark night of the soul'*, he told Miss Weaver in August.[436] He sought solace in drink and took up the familiar refrain that nobody understood him. 'Now Jim,' Nora would say, 'we've heard all that before.'[437]

Joyce could not really complain. *Finnegans Wake* was written to amuse James Joyce and it

In July 1927 Shakespeare & Company published Joyce's second poetry collection, *Pomes Penyeach*. Joyce hoped the 13 poems would be well received, but there was little interest. As Anthony Burgess has said, 'Joyce, a major poet in prose, was a very minor poet in verse. But he could be a very moving minor poet.'[438]

could be fully appreciated, on every level, only by James Joyce. He claimed he could *justify every line*, although he admitted that, as time went by, his grasp on the book became increasingly tenuous.[439] *We must do the job now before it is too late*, he said of a possible Italian translation, *for the moment there is at least one person, myself, who can understand what I am writing. I don't however guarantee that in two or three years I'll still be able to.*[440] He took great pains to decode sections of the book to his puzzled friends, *unconsciously explaining, for inkstands, with a meticulosity bordering on the insane, the various meanings of all the different foreign parts of speech he misused.*[441] Perhaps, as with *Ulysses*, he might have provided some key to the book, but his untimely death less than two years after the *Wake*'s publication leaves us guessing.

In 1927 he was visited by his old schoolfriend, Eugene Sheehy. Joyce immediately began 'naming former companions that I had well-nigh forgotten,' admits Sheehy, 'and he became quite impatient that I could not call to mind at once one Jack O'Reilly, who had faded from the Dublin scene for many years.'[442] Joyce's Dublin and the real thing were drifting further and further apart. In fact, much of the destruction of Joycean Dublin took place in his lifetime, while he was living abroad. When Sheehy remarked in passing that a statue had been moved from O'Connell Bridge, Joyce petulantly replied *Why has nobody told me that before?*[443]

Everything in Joyce's Paris *appartement* spelt 'Dublin', according to Sheehy. 'There were pictures and sketches of old Dublin on the walls, and even the design of the large rug, with which the floor was carpeted, portrayed the corkscrew course of the River Liffey.'[445] To Sheehy's sister, Joyce remarked: *There was an English queen who said that when she died the word 'Calais' would be written on her heart. 'Dublin' will be found on mine.*[446]

> 'I think *Finnegans Wake* rather represents a trap into which experimental writing can fall when it becomes purely experimental.'
> William S Burroughs[444]

In 1929 Joyce decided to answer his critics in a short essay collection published by Shakespeare & Company. He came up with the bizarre title *Our Exagmination round His Factification for Incamination of Work in Progress* and chose its 12 contributors (like the 12 apostles or the 12 customers in Mr Porter's pub) including Samuel Beckett, Frank Budgen and the poet William Carlos Williams (1883–1963). It ends with two comic letters of protest written in a sub-*Finnegan*ese.

In his essay, 'Dante . . . Bruno. Vico . . Joyce', Beckett claims *Work in Progress* as one of the few instances of pure self-expression in literature. If we find the language difficult it is because we are used to reading a transparent prose that doesn't draw attention to itself. (As Budgen says, 'our sensibilities have been steam-rollered flat by a vast bulk of

> Samuel Beckett (1906–89) was born in Foxrock, Ireland, and educated at Trinity College, Dublin. He befriended Joyce in Paris in 1928 and helped research *Work in Progress*. Famous for his plays *Waiting for Godot* (1955), *Endgame* (1958), *Krapp's Last Tape* (1958) and *Happy Days* (1961), Beckett actually preferred his novels, especially the trilogy *Molloy*, *Malone Dies* and *The Unnamable* (1951–3). His poem 'Home Olga' is an obscure acrostic on Joyce's name, probably written for Bloomsday 1932.

machine-made fiction.')[447] The English language has become too abstract and sophisticated over the centuries, says Beckett, so Joyce has 'desophisticated' it. The word 'doubt', for instance, conveys nothing of the extreme uncertainty of actually being in doubt. Joyce recognizes this and talks instead of being *in twosome twiminds*.[448] It is one small example of his desire to escape from the limitations of the English language. 'Here form *is* content, content *is* form,' says Beckett. 'You complain that this stuff is not written in English. It is not written at all. It is not to be read – or rather it is not only to be read. It is to be looked at and listened to. His writing is not *about* something; *it is that something itself*.'[449]

Beckett was a frequent visitor to the Joyce household and aided Joyce in his work. 'There wasn't a lot of conversation between us,' he later recounted. 'I was a young man, very devoted to him, and he liked me.'[450] Nothing grows in the shade, however. Beckett noted that his early writing 'stinks of Joyce in spite of most earnest endeavours to endow it with my own odours' and in 1932 he wrote 'I vow I will get over JJ ere I die. Yessir.'[451] He modified this view as his confidence in his own powers grew. A later entry in his journal reads: '[Joyce] was sublime last night, deprecating with the utmost conviction his lack of talent. I don't feel the danger of the association any more. He is just a very lovable human being.'[452]

Many who came within Joyce's orbit were overwhelmed by his personality. He was an arch coaxer and master manipulator with a shrewd understanding of human nature. 'He got people to put their time – and sometimes money – completely at his disposal,' said Stuart Gilbert, 'to follow him wherever he wanted them to accompany him; boring plays and operas, dull expensive restaurants; to [cancel] their arrangements if he wanted their assistance in some trivial, easily postponed task; to run errands for him, pull strings for him, undertake delicate and distasteful missions which exposed them to snubs, rebuffs and ridicules at his bidding.'[453]

Wedding day: *barnacled*

Beckett certainly felt drawn into a kind of Faustian pact and Joyce probably inspired the character of the blind tyrant Hamm in *Endgame* – Beckett being Clov, his put-upon servant. As Nora once said to Joyce, 'If God Almighty came down to earth, you'd have a job for him.'[454]

In November 1929 Joyce heard the French-Irish tenor John Sullivan at the Paris Opera and became an enthusiastic fan. In 1932 he would write 'From a Banned Writer to a Banned Singer', an attempt to further Sullivan's declining career, in which he complained that the tenor was banned (or at least unknown) in England. Writing in *Finnegan*ese, he puns on the names of operas, composers and singers and parodies 'God Save the King'.[455]

To the surprise of many, Joyce and Nora rented a flat in Kensington, London, in March 1930. He planned to marry Nora under English law (they were still British subjects) and needed an English address. Joyce had resisted marriage for 26 years. He regarded wedding rings as *symbols of slavery* and even forbade Nora to wear one for appearance's sake when she visited her family in 1912 (she did anyway).[456] Now, however, he wanted to legitimize Giorgio and Lucia in the eyes of the law, and marriage seemed the only option. In May he had a serious operation (his eleventh) to deal with a cataract on the left eye, but that year he still managed to produce another fragment of *Work in Progress, Haveth Childers Everywhere*, which incorporates more than 30 cities and place names and 60 mayors of Dublin.

Joyce claimed not to be interested in making money from his books, but he was not averse to a little self-publicity. In 1930 he chose somebody to write the story of his life. Herbert Gorman's biography, *James Joyce* (1939), with a little help from Joyce, emphasizes how much the Irishman had suffered for his art (Joyce calls it *the Martyrology of Gorman* in *Finnegans Wake*).[457] Also in 1930, Stuart Gilbert's *James Joyce's Ulysses* appeared, which explained (with substantial hints from Joyce) the complex grid of allusions in the novel. The Joyce industry had begun.

James Joyce and Nora Barnacle were married on 4 July 1931 (his father's birthday). Now he was *barnacled up to the eyes*, as he puts it in *Finnegans Wake*.[458] They went to great lengths to keep the ceremony secret; but when they emerged from Kensington register office the press lay in wait. Joyce was appalled, though privately he enjoyed the attention and made sure to collect all the newspaper cuttings.

'My first impression is of a slightly bearded spinster,' wrote the diarist Harold Nicolson (1886–1968) after meeting Joyce in

London. The famous author of *Ulysses* also reminded him of 'some thin little bird, peeking, crooked, reserved, violent and timid. Little claw hands. So blind that he stares away from one at a tangent, like a very thin owl.' He concluded that 'Joyce manages to hide his dislike of the English in general and of the literary English in particular. But he is a difficult man to talk to.'[459] This depended on the company. In Paris that same year his schoolfriend William Fallon found Joyce extremely talkative and 'preoccupied with memories of Dublin'.[460] He remembered Fallon's old house in Fitzwilliam Street and could name and number every dwelling on both sides of the street from memory. 'Joyce's memory for detail . . . was extraordinary,' said Fallon. 'He recalled how he had exchanged whispers with the little Italian boy on his first day in Belvedere. He described our classroom with the crucifix over the fireplace, and listed, without hesitation, a score of boy's names in our class.'[461] There is something rather poignant about the 49-year-old Joyce asking after the boys he used to play Red Indians with or requesting Fallon to do his imitation of their maths teacher. As another friend noted, Joyce 'cannot forget Dublin, cannot forget schooldays, and childhood'.[462]

In the Dublin of my day there was the kind of desperate freedom which comes from a lack of responsibility, for the English were in governance then, so everyone said what he liked. Now I hear since the Free State came in there is less freedom. The Church has made inroads everywhere, so that we are in fact becoming a bourgeois nation, with the Church supplying our aristocracy . . . and I do not see much hope for us intellectually.[463]

James Joyce

But Dublin had changed in Joyce's absence. It was no longer the city he had so carefully preserved in *Ulysses*. He was forced to accept this unpalatable fact when his father died on 29 December 1931. Joyce could not bring himself to attend the funeral for a host of reasons. He felt that returning to Dublin would make it impossible for him to write about it in *Finnegans Wake*, but he also did not want his arrival to be seen as an endorsement of the new Irish Free State, of which he remained sceptical. Nor had he forgotten his last visit to Dublin. As he says in *Finnegans Wake*: *Our durlbin is sworming in sneaks.*[464] When he added up all these misgivings, he sometimes wondered why he was writing about Dublin at all. *Why go on writing about a place I did not dare to go to at such a moment, where not three persons know me or understand me.*[465]

Joyce with his son Giorgio and grandson Stephen

Two months after John Joyce's death, Giorgio's wife gave birth to a boy, Stephen James, and Joyce became a grandfather. Joy broke in on his grief and he turned to poetry to express himself. 'Ecce Puer', his best poem, is a fitting conclusion to his career as a poet and he made sure to add it to his *Collected Poems* (1936).[466] Despite this happy news Joyce was sliding into depression. He was miserable for much of the time and sought solace in *Work in Progress*. *Life is so tragic*, he wrote to a friend, *birth, death, departure (separation), sickness, death, that we are permitted to distract ourselves and forget a little.*[467]

One of his major concerns was Lucia, now a young woman of 25, although Joyce still treated her like a child. He believed her when she said she had been seduced by the young men who visited him and sent them away (including Samuel Beckett, who was briefly an unwilling object of Lucia's affections). When the

Troubled: Lucia Joyce

psychologist Carl Jung pointed out certain schizoid characteristics in Lucia's letters, Joyce insisted that they anticipated a new kind of literature, like his own experiments with the language. But in the end her erratic behaviour could no longer be attributed to high spirits and in 1932 Lucia began to show signs of schizophrenia. Joyce blamed himself: *Whatever spark of gift I possess has been transmitted to Lucia, and has kindled a fire in her brain.*[468]

He took it upon himself to cure her and began by buying her an expensive fur coat. *I think that will do her inferiority complex more good than a visit to a psychoanalyst*, he said.[469] He also encouraged her to design decorative initial letters, which he had published in *A Chaucer ABC* (1936). And so began a battle with psychoanalytic orthodoxy for which, in the final assessment, Joyce was poorly equipped. It was as if he expected a miracle. He even hoped that finishing *Finnegans Wake* would put an end to his daughter's instability, as if she suffered from too close a proximity to his literary experiment. He was, as psychologists say, in denial.

On the other hand, Joyce's refusal to give up on Lucia and have her institutionalized is entirely commendable. He regarded psychoanalysis as little more than blackmail and was adamant that he could learn as much from himself as from a so-called expert (*I can psoakoonaloose myself any time I want*).[470] His dream interpretations show the influence of Freud, but he found psychoanalytic symbolism too mechanical. It lacked the subtlety he sought in *Finnegans Wake*.

Lucia's behaviour became increasingly strange and at times violent. Nora insisted they could no longer cope and Joyce reluctantly agreed. Lucia was sent to a nursing home at Ivry, just outside Paris, where he would visit her every week without fail. He was convinced she would get better and in 1937 he wrote to a friend that she was *at last on the road to recovery*.[471] It proved a false hope. In 1951 Lucia was transferred to St Andrew's Hospital in Northampton, England, where she died in 1982.

The strain of writing *Finnegans Wake* and his worries about Lucia made him drink more heavily. He also had constant trouble with his eyes and suffered from insomnia and in January 1933 he added stomach cramps to his list of ailments. His doctor attributed these attacks to nerves and prescribed laudanum. The real cause would not be diagnosed until January 1941, by which time it was too late.

In the mid-1930s Joyce cut a sorry, even tragic figure, yet somehow he still found the energy to work almost every day on his *Work in Progress*. In June 1934 *The Mime of Mick Nick and the Maggies* was published. It ends: *Loud, heap miseries upon us yet entwine our arts with laughters low.*[472] Around this time Harold

Nicolson visited Joyce's flat in the rue Galilée. 'It is a little furnished flat,' he observed, 'as stuffy and prim as a hotel bedroom. [Joyce] glided in. It was evident he had just been shaving. He was very spruce and nervous and chatty. Great rings upon little twitching fingers. Huge concave spectacles which flicked reflections of the lights as he moved his head like a bird, turning it with the definite insistence to the speaker as blind people do who turn to the sound of a voice . . . He was very courteous, as shy people are. His beautiful voice trilled on slowly like Anna Livia Plurabelle. He has the most lovely voice I know – liquid and soft with undercurrents of gurgle . . . My impression [was] of a very nervous and refined animal – a gazelle in a drawing-room. His blindness increases that impression. I suppose he is a real person somewhere, but I feel that I have never spent half-an-hour with anyone and been left with an impression of such brittle and vulnerable strangeness.'[473]

On 6 December 1933 the US trial of *Ulysses* came to an end. 'My considered opinion,' said Justice John M Woolsey, the federal district judge in New York, 'is that whilst in many places the effect of *Ulysses* on the reader undoubtedly is somewhat emetic, nowhere does it tend to be an aphrodisiac. *Ulysses* may, therefore, be admitted to the United States.'[474] Random House published it in January 1934 and that same month the 51-year-old Joyce appeared on the front cover of *Time*. 'Is it dirty?' asked the magazine of *Ulysses*. 'Yes,' but it was also 'one of the most monumental works of the human intelligence.' Posterity would judge, it added, but Joyce had probably robbed the language of the word 'unprintable'.[475]

In Britain, John Lane of The Bodley Head tested the situation by posting a copy of *Ulysses* from Paris to his London address – it got through. Encouraged, he decided to publish it, although the book was delayed for two years because the printers objected to certain passages. It was not until October 1936 that 1,000 copies of *Ulysses* went on sale in London. There was brisk demand and Joyce was more than satisfied by the news. *Now the war between England and me is over*, he said, *and I am the conqueror.*[476]

The Home Office regarded the publication of a British edition as 'extremely awkward', because the ban had not been lifted. True, *Ulysses* was so expensive it would not 'get into the hands of anyone likely to be corrupted by it', but there was the risk of a cheaper edition later. At a hastily convened Whitehall conference in November 1936 it was agreed no action should be taken to prosecute The Bodley Head. 'Standards in these matters are constantly changing,' admitted the Attorney-General and *Ulysses* had an 'established position in literature'. Joyce had indeed won.

Throughout 1937 Joyce lived quietly, working on *Finnegans Wake*. He calculated that he wrote about 16 hours a day, often late into the night (Nora could hear him chuckling over it). In 1938 he offered his friends 1,000 French francs if they could guess the title of his new book, which he had not even vouchsafed to his publishers, Faber and Faber. He was stunned when Eugene Jolas finally came up with *Finnegans Wake*, but promptly delivered the money in person the next day.

Joyce's long labour of love was coming to an end and he thought very hard about the last word of *Finnegans Wake*, just as he had over the final *Yes* of *Ulysses*. Eventually he decided it should end with the word 'the': *the most slippery, the least accented, the weakest word in English, a word which is not even a word, which is scarcely sounded between the teeth, a breath, a nothing.*[477]

One afternoon in November 1938 he completed the last section, in which Anna Livia expresses her sorrow at having to die (as the River Liffey runs into Dublin Bay), but accepts her place within the Viconian cycle of death and rebirth. Joyce, too, seems to be signing off. Did he know it would be his last book? *I am passing out. O bitter ending! I'll slip away before they're up. They'll never see. Nor know. Nor miss me. And it's old and old it's sad and old it's sad and weary I go back to you, my cold father, my cold mad father, my cold mad feary father . . .* [478]

He left the flat feeling *completely exhausted, as if all the blood had run out of my brain* and sat on a bench for a long time *unable to move.*[479] By sundown his spirits had revived and he allowed himself a little self-congratulation and a large drink.

As usual, Joyce wanted his new book to be delivered on his birthday and barely slept in order to read over the proofs in time. On 30 January 1939 a copy arrived from Faber and Faber and Joyce was delighted. His fifty-seventh birthday party on 2 February was suitably grand and was dominated by an enormous cake in the shape of seven books iced in the colour of their bindings: *Chamber Music, Dubliners, A Portrait of the Artist as a Young Man, Exiles, Ulysses, Pomes Penyeach* and *Finnegans Wake*. After dinner Giorgio sang a duet with his father and there was a reading of the last pages of *Finnegans Wake*. Joyce had a splendid time, but afterwards his spirits drooped. He loved the experience of living with a book and throwing all of his considerable energies into it, but he no longer had a project to play with and political events in Europe were beginning to overshadow everything else. *War is going to break out*, he complained, *and nobody will be reading my book any more.*[480] All wars achieved nothing in his view, they were simply part of the cycle of history, as he had tried to show in *Finnegans Wake*.

Unlike Pound or Wyndham Lewis, Joyce was immune to *poor Mr Hitler-Missler* and in 1938 he had helped the Austrian novelist Hermann Broch (1886–1951) and others escape from Nazi-held territory.[481] On the whole, however, he did not want to be dragged into politics. After all, many of his Dublin friends had paid a high price for their political convictions. Clancy, who had become Lord Mayor of Limerick, had been murdered by the Black and Tans. During the Easter Rising, Skeffington had organized a Citizen's Defence Force to prevent looting, but had been arrested and shot by a firing squad at the command of a British captain who was later declared insane (Skeffington's widow refused the £10,000 offered in compensation). Kettle had fought in the British Army in the First World War in the vain hope Britain would reward Irish help by granting Ireland independence. He was killed leading his company of Dublin Fusiliers at the Somme.

Finnegans Wake was published in May and Joyce pored over the reviews. They were, on the whole, disappointing as reviewers struggled to make any sense of it. He had suffered indignities in the past, but the hostile reception of *Finnegans Wake* was of another order. The rumour

Shem the Penman, 1932. Joyce photographed by Josef Breitenbach

circulated that he had been spoiled by fame and that now, surrounded by sycophants and yes-men, he no longer knew what he was doing and his talent had been ruined. As Jung commented, 'In any other time of the past [*Finnegans Wake*] would never have reached the printer, but in our blessed XXth century it is a message, though not yet understood.'[482]

War was declared in September and the blackout made it impossible for Joyce to negotiate the streets of Paris alone at night. Their friends were leaving and the Joyces moved from their flat to a hotel. In December they spent Christmas with friends in the French village of Saint-Gérand-le-Puy, where they stayed until the spring. Joyce was morose and taciturn, though occasionally he revived and would sing and dance. But most of all he liked to lie on the bed, smoking and thinking over his next book. It was going to be *very simple and very short*.[483] He hinted to Stanislaus that after the *Wake* there would be a sequel, a reawakening – it is a tantalising glimpse of what might have been.

In April 1940 Joyce and Nora moved to a hotel in Vichy. After the deceptive calm of the Phoney War came the dramatic Fall of France. Giorgio was still in Paris in May when the Nazis invaded and his parents were concerned for his safety. Paris fell on 14 June and Joyce and Nora returned to Saint-Gérand-le-Puy. Giorgio appeared there too, having fled Paris in the exodus. Samuel Beckett (later an active member of the French Resistance) also passed through the village and this was the last time he saw Joyce.

The Nazis briefly occupied Saint-Gérand-le-Puy and the Joyces stayed indoors, listening to the wireless for news of Paris, where they hoped to return. In the midst of all this drama and tension Joyce was still correcting typos in *Finnegans Wake* with the help of his Russian-Jewish friend Paul Léon. Against Joyce's advice, Léon returned to Occupied Paris and rescued some of Joyce's books and papers from his flat. They were sent to Dublin via the Irish Ambassador to Occupied France with strict instructions from Léon that they should not be opened until 50 years after Joyce's death.[484]

Joyce was not a well man and in September 1940 he made plans to move to Switzerland, preferably Zurich. He always favoured Europe over the United States; besides, he was well known in Zurich, having been a refugee there during the First World War, but for some reason the Swiss refused him an entry visa, possibly because it was rumoured he was Jewish. It took several applications before the Swiss authorities acknowledged him as a British citizen (Joyce had been offered Irish citizenship that year and had politely but firmly refused) and in November Joyce, Nora and

Friends: Joyce and Paul Léon, Paris, 1936

Giorgio were issued with the necessary visas. Further obstacles were placed in their way by the new Vichy government (1940–44) and they were forbidden to leave because their passports had expired.

On top of all these difficulties, Joyce had a greater worry: Lucia was still in a nursing home in what was now Occupied France. He refused to abandon her, but in the end he was forced to, despite his best efforts to have her transferred to a Swiss clinic. At 3 a.m. on 14 December, tired and defeated, he boarded a train bound for Geneva with Nora, Giorgio and Stephen. On 17 December they arrived at a hotel in wintry Zurich. Joyce had no interest in anything and looked much older than his 58 years.

He spent a lot of time with his grandson, walking through the snow and telling him tales from the *Odyssey*. Occasionally he would stop and produce a little black notebook, place it on the boy's back and scribble something. This notebook has never been found, so we will probably never know what exercised Joyce's mind in these final weeks.

On 9 January 1941 he suffered terrible stomach cramps and early in the morning a doctor was called. He was taken by ambulance to a hospital in great pain, despite doses of morphine. An X-ray revealed a perforated duodenal ulcer. On 11 January he was operated on and recovered consciousness. *I thought I wouldn't get through it*, he admitted to Nora.[485] He revived a little, but was worse the next morning and by the afternoon was in a coma.

According to his sister Eva, Joyce's last words were 'Does nobody understand?' – an uncanny echo of Anna Livia's dying words in *Finnegans Wake*: *I done my best when I was let. Thinking always if I go all goes. A hundred cares, a tithe of troubles and is there one who understands me?*[486] But Eva was not present at Joyce's death. Tragically, Nora and Giorgio had gone home to get some rest, reassured that his condition was stable. At 1 a.m. on 13 January 1941 Joyce awoke and asked for his wife and son, before again losing consciousness. He died alone at 2.15 a.m. If he had any last words for posterity, they were lost on the hospital staff.

A sculptor made two death masks of Joyce's face and he was buried on 15 January 1941. Nora declined the offer of a Catholic burial, saying 'I couldn't do that to him.'[487] Although there were two senior Irish diplomats present in Switzerland at the time, neither troubled to attend Joyce's funeral. At the service in Fluntern Cemetery, the tenor Max Meili sang '*Addio terra, addio cielo*' ('Farewell earth, farewell sky') from the second act of Monteverdi's *Orfeo* (1607). Lord Derwent, the British minister to Bern, delivered the eulogy 'Hail and Farewell'. 'Of all the injustices Britain has heaped upon Ireland,' he said, 'Ireland will continue to enjoy the lasting revenge of producing masterpieces of English literature.'[488]

I am passing out. O bitter ending!

Nora Joyce died ten years after her husband on 10 April 1951 and was buried in a separate plot because there was no room next to Joyce. In June 1966 their remains were exhumed and they were finally reunited in what has become a much-visited *Ehrengrab* or 'grave of honour'.

When Lucia was told about her father's death, she refused to believe it. 'What is he doing under the ground, that idiot?' she asked. 'When will he decide to come out? He's watching us all the time.'[489] It was as if Joyce, like Finn MacCool, were merely sleeping until his time came round again.

Envoy: mememormee!

Samuel Beckett has spoken of 'Joyce's heroic achievement . . . That's what it was epic, heroic, what he achieved.'[490] This cannot be denied, but what was Joyce's legacy?

In Dublin his image is used to sell the city to the world. As one critic has observed, 'the Joyce cult . . . is a useful adjunct to the Irish tourist industry, though Joyce could hardly be thought a typical Irishman, unless it is typically Irish to spend most of one's life abroad, unpublished in Ireland.'[491]

It took a long time for the prodigal son to return. 'The Irish didn't want to know about him,' says Ken Monaghan, a nephew of Joyce and cultural director of Dublin's James Joyce Centre, 'it was almost a curse to be a Joyce.'[492] In 1993 Joyce's face appeared on the Irish £10 note (on the back were the opening lines of *Finnegans Wake*). It was a sure sign of his rehabilitation, although he was replaced by the euro in 2002. A committed Europhile, Joyce would no doubt have savoured this irony.

The International Joyce Foundation has criticized Dublin city council for allowing many of the buildings and bars mentioned by Joyce to lie derelict or become tacky theme pubs. Few of Joyce's Dublin homes carry a commemorative plaque and many have been demolished. In 2003 there was an outcry when the council announced plans to pull down one of the last surviving brothels in Monto (Nighttown) and replace it with an arts and community centre.

In 1923 the American novelist F Scott Fitzgerald (1896–1940) predicted that Joyce would be 'the most profound literary influence in the next fifty years'.[493] He was right. As the critic D J Taylor has observed: '*Ulysses*'s grandiloquent wordplay, exuberant dramatisations and rapt interior monologues spread through the mid-century English novel like loosestrife through a hedge.'[494]

Joyce's influence can be felt in Evelyn Waugh's *Decline and Fall* (1928) and *Vile Bodies* (1930), in George Orwell's *A Clergyman's Daughter* (1935) and Virginia Woolf's *Mrs Dalloway* (1925). One might add to this list the works of Jorge Luis Borges (1899–1986), Vladimir Nabokov (1899–1977), Raymond Queneau (1903–76), Anthony Burgess (1917–93), Italo Calvino (1923–85), Philip K Dick (1928–82), Umberto Eco (*b*.1932), Philip Roth (*b*.1933), Georges Perec (1936–82), Thomas Pynchon (*b*.1937) and many others. Samuel Beckett, of course, fell under his spell, but went in the opposite direction. 'I realised that Joyce had gone as far as one could in the direction of knowing more,' he said. 'I realised that my own way was in impoverishment, in lack of knowledge and in taking away, in subtracting rather than adding.'[495]

In the 1950s the so-called *nouveau roman* ('new novel') movement rejected the idea that a novel must have a subject, characters and a plot. Rebelling against the psychological novel, writers like Nathalie Sarraute (1900–99) and Alain Robbe-Grillet (*b*.1922) argued that the novelist should not try to get inside the head of a character, but should be concerned only with the outside. The novel should be a systematized and analytical record of objects and things. It might be assumed that Joyce – the greatest exponent of the 'stream of consciousness' technique – would be out of favour, but in fact he was a major influence, albeit the Joyce of 'Ithaca' rather than 'Penelope'.

In the late 1960s a new movement, post-structuralism, signalled a fresh self-consciousness about language and meaning, with *Finnegans Wake* as its anti-Bible. It has even been suggested that without Joyce post-structuralism might never have happened. Post-structuralists celebrated the irreducible excesses of language as a multiple play of meaning and in their view Joyce's punning distortions fractured the unity of the word as a stable sign. His slippery *Finneganese* undermines all attempts to grasp its meaning once and for all and this subversive free play of infinite plurality appealed to post-structuralists.

The French philosopher Jacques Derrida (*b*.1930) – a major figure in post-structuralism – admits to being haunted by Joyce and by the feeling that anything he might write has already been read in advance by *Finnegans Wake*, 'because you can say nothing that is not programmed on this 1000th generation computer'.[496] According to Derrida, it is ludicrous to say 'I have read Joyce', because we are always on the edge of reading him. As Joyce once said: *The demand that I make of my reader is that he should devote his whole life to reading my works.*[497]

Some critics accuse Joyce of being an insufferable egotist, but others, like the French composer Pierre Boulez (*b*.1925), have argued that Joyce's fiction is actually marked by the pursuit of anonymity. According to Boulez, *Ulysses* and *Finnegans Wake* herald 'a new age in which texts are becoming, as it were, "anonymous", "speaking for themselves without any author's voice".'[498] As Stephen says in *A Portrait*: *The narrative is no longer purely personal. The personality of the artist passes into the narration itself, flowing round and round the persons and the action like a vital sea . . . The artist, like the God of the creation, remains within or behind or beyond or above his handiwork, invisible, refined out of existence, indifferent, paring his fingernails.*[500]

'Someday I'm going to get my article published; I'm going to prove that *Finnegans Wake* is an information pool based on computer memory systems that didn't exist until centuries after James Joyce's era; that Joyce was plugged into a cosmic consciousness from which he derived the inspiration for his entire corpus of work.'
Philip K Dick, *The Divine Invasion*[499]

Notes

The following works are referred to by the abbreviations below.

D   James Joyce, *Dubliners* (1914), ed Jeri Johnson (Oxford: Oxford University Press, 2000)

FW   James Joyce, *Finnegans Wake* (1939; repr. London: Faber and Faber, 1960)

JJ   Richard Ellmann, *James Joyce* (1959; rev. edn. Oxford: Oxford University Press, 1983)

P   James Joyce, *A Portrait of the Artist as a Young Man* (1916), ed Jeri Johnson (Oxford: Oxford University Press, 2000)

PSW   James Joyce, *Poems and Shorter Writings*, ed Richard Ellmann, A Walton Litz and John Whittier-Ferguson (1991; repr. London: Faber and Faber, 2001)

SH   James Joyce, *Stephen Hero*, ed Theodore Spencer (1944); rev. edn., eds John J Slocum and Herbert Cahoon (St Albans: Triad/Panther, 1977)

SL   *Selected Letters of James Joyce*, ed Richard Ellmann (1975; repr. London: Faber and Faber, 1992)

U   James Joyce, *Ulysses* (1922), ed Jeri Johnson (1993; repr. Oxford: Oxford University Press, 1998)

1   *SL* 360–61.
2   *The Joyce We Knew*, ed Ulick O'Connor (Cork: The Mercier Press, 1967), p.26.
3   Ibid., p.22.
4   *P* 5.
5   *P* 203.
6   *P* 74.
7   *The Joyce We Knew*, p.9.
8   *JJ* 661.
9   *The Joyce We Knew*, pp.23–4.
10   James Joyce, *Occasional, Critical, and Political Writing*, ed Kevin Barry (Oxford: Oxford University Press, 2000) pp.191, 240.
11   Ibid., p.195.
12   *P* 204.
13   *P* 16; 11.
14   *P* 41.
15   *JJ* 30.
16   *Occasional, Critical, and Political Writing*, pp.194, 142.

17   *PSW* 103.
18   *P* 28.
19   *D* 103. Only a few lines of 'Et Tu, Healy' have survived (see *PSW* 71). Joyce parodies its *tumtum* rhythm in *Finnegans Wake* (*FW* 231.5–8).
20   *P* 28. Mrs Hearn Conway (the model for Dante (meaning 'Auntie') Riordan in *A Portrait*) came from Cork and was Joyce's governess. She had two hair-brushes: one maroon for Davitt and his Land League, the other green for Parnell. When Parnell was declared an adulterer she ripped off the green backing (*P* 12).
21   *P* 31.
22   *P* 170.
23   *SL* 27. The friend in question was J F Byrne.
24   *SL* 25.
25   *P* 55.

26 *P* 54–5.

27 *P* 55.

28 *P* 65–6.

29 *P* 131. There is an affectionate portrait of Father Conmee in the 'Wandering Rocks' episode of *Ulysses* (*U* 210ff).

30 *The Joyce We Knew*, p.15.

31 Ibid., p.46.

32 Ibid., p.65.

33 Ibid., p.29.

34 *SL* 293.

35 All quotations from Charles and Mary Lamb's *The Adventures of Ulysses* are taken from the Juvenile Library edition (London, 1808).

36 *D* 19. It was long thought that the Joyces lived at number 17, but it seems likely it was number 13, where a Father Quaid died.

37 *JJ* 418.

38 *U* 271.

39 *JJ* 347.

40 *JJ* 47.

41 *P* 83.

42 *U* 570.

43 As recalled by Stephen in *Ulysses* p.530: *Queens lay with prize bulls. Remember Pasiphae for whose lust my grandoldgrossfather made the first confessionbox.*

44 *FW* 32.26.

45 *FW* 220.24.

46 *P* 205. The extent and nature of Joyce's religious belief has been hotly debated, but perhaps the last word should go to Joyce himself. In May 1905 he wrote to Stanislaus from Trieste about an English teacher at the Berlitz School: *He says I will die a Catholic because I am always moping in and out of Greek churches and am a believer at heart: whereas in my opinion I am incapable of belief of any kind.* (*SL* 62)

47 *P* 142.

48 *P* 143.

49 *P* 144.

50 *P*144–5; perhaps an echo of the last line of Alfred Lord Tennyson's 'Ulysses'

(1833): 'To strive, to seek, to find, and not to yield.'

51 *P* 66.

52 *U* 184.

53 *FW* 182.13–14.

54 *The Joyce We Knew*, p.58.

55 *P* 77–8.

56 *P* 56.

57 *P* 55.

58 *The Joyce We Knew*, p.27.

59 *P* 147–8.

60 *P* 181.

61 *The Joyce We Knew*, pp.52–3.

62 *JJ* 382.

63 Quoted in Dominic Manganiello, *Joyce's Politics* (London: Routledge & Kegan Paul, 1980), p.144.

64 *Occasional, Critical, and Political Writing*, p.4.

65 See 'Reflections on *Vers Libre*' in *Selected Prose of T S Eliot*, ed. Frank Kermode (London: Faber and Faber, 1984), pp.31–6.

66 Ezra Pound on *Ulysses*, in *Literary Essays of Ezra Pound*, ed T S Eliot (1954; repr. London: Faber and Faber, 1963), p.408.

67 *SH* 76.

68 *Occasional, Critical, and Political Writing*, p.28.

69 Ibid.

70 *SH* 76.

71 *SH* 79.

72 *SH* 35.

73 *SH* 85.

74 *SH* 83.

75 *SH* 86.

76 *SH* 90.

77 *SH* 95.

78 *SH* 42.

79 *JJ* 73.

80 *Occasional, Critical, and Political Writing*, p.31.

81 *SL* 6.

82 *SL* 7.

83 *U* 548.

84 *SH* 188. In *Ulysses*, Leopold Bloom lives

on Eccles Street.

85 Ibid. Stephen recalls his *epiphanies on green oval leaves* in *Ulysses*, amused at their self-conscious seriousness (*U* 41). See also 'Epiphanies' (*PSW* 155–200).

86 *JJ* 102.

87 *P* 147.

88 *D* 130.

89 *Occasional, Critical, and Political Writing*, p.50.

90 *JJ* 153

91 *Occasional, Critical, and Political Writing*, p.60.

92 *The Collected Poems of W B Yeats* (London: Macmillan, 1985), pp.48–9.

93 *SH* 148.

94 Ibid.

95 *SH* 149.

96 *JJ* 132.

97 *PSW* 180.

98 *JJ* 100–1.

99 *U* 182.

100 Quoted in Bernard McGinley, *Joyce's Lives: Uses and Abuses of the Biografiend* (London: University of North London Press, 1996), p.28.

101 *JJ* 104.

102 *SL* 8.

103 *P* 213. In August 1912, Joyce wrote to his future wife Nora Barnacle: *I am one of the writers of this generation who are perhaps creating at last a conscience in the soul of this wretched race.* (*SL* 204)

104 James Joyce, *The Essential James Joyce*, ed Harry Levin (1948; repr. London: Triad Paladin, 1985), p.427.

105 *P* 206.

106 *U* 26.

107 *SL* 14.

108 *JJ* 125.

109 *U* 43.

110 Ibid.

111 *JJ* 132.

112 *U* 42. See also *U* 787n.

113 *U* 6.

114 *P* 203–4.

115 *U* 5.

116 *SL* 25.

117 *U* 41.

118 *The Joyce We Knew*, p.68.

119 *U* 4.

120 *U* 5.

121 *D* 34.

122 *The Joyce We Knew*, p.8.

123 Ibid. p.9.

124 Ibid.

125 *PSW* 203.

126 *SL* 161.

127 *SL* 21.

128 *SL* 159.

129 See Joyce's recollection of the event in his letter to Nora of 3 December 1909 (*SL* 181–3).

130 *U* 209.

131 *SL* 21.

132 *SL* 28.

133 *SL* 25–6.

134 *FW* 184.4.

135 Bernard O'Donoghue in *Oxford Poetry* Vol VI, No 1 (Summer 1991), p.31.

136 *JJ* 660–1n.

137 *SL* 22.

138 *U* 185.

139 *PSW* 97.

140 *SL* 129.

141 *PSW* 98.

142 *SL* 51; 70.

143 *PSW* 99.

144 *PSW* 29.

145 *JJ* 277. Gogarty is referred to in lines 31–2 of 'The Holy Office'.

146 *JJ* 174.

147 *JJ* 207.

148 *U* 4.

149 *SL* 30.

150 Ibid.

151 Quoted in Brenda Maddox, *Nora: A Biography of Nora Joyce* (1988; repr. London: Minerva, 1990), p.63.

152 *SL* 32.

153 *D* 29.

154 Some chapter titles are taken from

Joyce's work: *self exiled in upon his ego* comes from *Finnegans Wake* (*FW* 184.6–7). OMINOUS – FOR HIM! comes from *Ulysses* (*U* 137). Litterarum Anglicarum Pontifex Maximus ('High Priest of English Letters') is a phrase that appears in abbreviated form at the end one of Joyce's letters, postmarked 29 August 1920 (*SL* 268). *O! Infamy!* comes from *Ulysses* (*U* 513). *The Strangest Dream that was ever Halfdreamt* comes from *Finnegans Wake* (*FW* 307.11–12), as do *inkbattle* (*FW* 176.31) and *mememormee!* (*FW* 628.14), which combines not only 'Remember me!' (the words of the ghost of Hamlet's father) but 'memory', 'memorial' and also the rather egotistical 'me, me – more me!'

155 *SL* 56.
156 *SL* 45.
157 See *P* 75.
158 *SL* 66.
159 *SL* 76.
160 *SL* 71.
161 *JJ* 204.
162 *SL* 70.
163 *SL* 80–1.
164 *SL* 82, 89–90.
165 *SL* 112.
166 *SL* 153.
167 *SL* 121.
168 *SL* 161.
169 Ezra Pound, 'Joyce' (*The Future*, May 1918) in *Literary Essays of Ezra Pound*, p.413.
170 *Joyce's Politics*, p.145.
171 *SL* 168.
172 *SL* 142.
173 *SL* 131.
174 *SL* 145.
175 *SL* 161.
176 *D* 169.
177 *D* 174.
178 *D* 176.
179 Ibid.

180 *PSW* 54.
181 James Joyce, *Exiles: A Play in Three Acts* with Joyce's Notes and an Introduction by Padraic Colum (London: Jonathan Cape, 1952), p.167.
182 *SL* 151.
183 *JJ* 241.
184 *Occasional, Critical, and Political Writing*, p.139. See also Stephen's comment in *A Portrait* that Irish nationalism always produces *the indispensable informer.* (*P* 169)
185 *Occasional, Critical, and Political Writing*, p.140.
186 *JJ* 238.
187 It was not until 2000 that the original Italian texts of Joyce's articles were made available – at the insistence of the James Joyce Estate – in *Occasional, Critical, and Political Writings*.
188 *Occasional, Critical, and Political Writing*, p.123. His other lectures were 'James Clarence Mangan' and another on the Irish Literary Renaissance. See *Occasional, Critical, and Political Writing*, pp.127–37.
189 *JJ* 446.
190 *FW* 72.16–17.
191 *FW* 540.26–7.
192 *JJ* 260.
193 *JJ* 437.
194 *JJ* 266.
195 *JJ* 268.
196 *Occasional, Critical, and Political Writing*, pp.148–151, 233–37.
197 *SL* 156.
198 *SL* 157.
199 *SL* 156.
200 Ibid.
201 *SL* 158–9.
202 *SL* 160.
203 *SL* 163.
204 *JJ* 291.
205 B S Johnson, *Aren't You Rather Young To Be Writing Your Memoirs?* (London: Hutchinson, 1973), p.11.

206 *SL* 174.

207 *SL* 188.

208 *SL* 169.

209 *JJ* 308.

210 *SL* 193.

211 See *D* 251n102.10. Joyce eventually changed it to *his old mother* (*D* 102). Mr O'Connor says *Why should we welcome the King of England?* (*D* 102) and Joe Hynes says *What do we want kowtowing to a foreign king?* (*D* 94).

212 There is some disagreement whether it was the manuscript of *A Portrait* that Joyce consigned to the flames – it might have been the first draft of *Stephen Hero*.

213 *U* 36.

214 *SL* 202–3.

215 *JJ* 331.

216 *SL* 205.

217 *SL* 206.

218 *JJ* 337.

219 Quoted in Frank Budgen, *James Joyce and the Making of 'Ulysses'* (1934; repr. Bloomington: Indiana University Press, 1960), pp.67–8.

220 *PSW* 104–5.

221 *PSW* 229, 235.

222 *PSW* 231.

223 *PSW* 240.

224 'A Flower Given to My Daughter' appeared in *Pomes Penyeach* (1927). See *PSW* 53 and the line in *Giacomo Joyce*: *A flower given by her to my daughter. Frail gift, frail giver, frail blue-veined child.* (*PSW* 230)

225 *The Essential James Joyce*, pp.435–6.

226 Michael Billington, *The Life and Work of Harold Pinter* (London: Faber and Faber, 1997), p.209–11.

227 Ezra Pound, '*Dubliners* and Mr James Joyce' (15 July 1914) in *Literary Essays of Ezra Pound*, pp.399–402.

228 *P* 213.

229 *JJ* 383.

230 *JJ* 420.

231 *JJ* 417.

232 *SL* 219–20.

233 Hans Arp, quoted in Hans Richter, *Dada: Art and Anti-Art* (London: Thames and Hudson, 1997), p.25.

234 *JJ* 404.

235 *James Joyce: The Critical Heritage*, Volume I, ed Robert H Deming (London: Routledge & Kegan Paul, 1970), pp.102, 86.

236 *Literary Essays of Ezra Pound*, p.410–15.

237 *JJ* 416.

238 Ezra Pound to James Joyce, 19 December 1917, in *Pound/Joyce: The Letters of Ezra Pound to James Joyce, with Pound's Essays on Joyce*, ed Forrest Read (London: Faber and Faber, 1968), p.129.

239 *JJ* 426.

240 Quoted by Alan Travis in *Bound and Gagged: A Secret History of Obscenity in Britain* (London: Profile Books, 2000), p.19.

241 *SL* 239; *U* 291; *FW* 416.3.

242 Rayner Heppenstall in 'Ulysses Returns', *The Modern Movement: A TLS Companion*, ed John Goss (London: Harvill, 1992) pp.62–3.

243 *JJ* 451.

244 *JJ* 445.

245 *U* 74.

246 Bloom breaks wind on p.279 of *Ulysses*.

247 *U* 293.

248 *Occasional, Critical, and Political Writing*, pp.138, 237; *U* 293–7.

249 *JJ* 399; *U* 549: *But I say: Let my country die for me.*

250 *JJ* 462.

251 *JJ* 472.

252 *SL* 246.

253 *JJ* 475.

254 *Absinthe the lot*, but *Rome boose for the Bloom toff* (*U* 405).

255 *SL* 251–2.

256 *JJ* 476; *SL* 241. The artist Richard Hamilton's treatment of this episode is inspired. *In Horne's House* (1949, rev. 1981) depicts a sequence of artistic

styles from the earliest origins of art to the art of the twentieth century. See *Imaging Ulysses: Richard Hamilton's Illustrations to James Joyce* (London: The British Council, Visual Arts Publications, 2002).

257 *SL* 265.

258 *Letters of James Joyce*, Volume III, ed Richard Ellmann (London: Faber and Faber, 1966), p.22.

259 *JJ* 492.

260 *SL* 283.

261 *SL* 271n (translation). The full Linati Schema, as well as the Gorman–Gilbert Plan, can be found in the OUP edition of *Ulysses*, ed Jeri Johnson (*U* 734–9), and also in Richard Ellmann, *Ulysses on the Liffey* (London: Faber and Faber, 1984) between pp.188–9.

262 *SL* 274.

263 *JJ* 519.

264 *JJ* 521.

265 *JJ* 516. In the 'Hades' episode, Bloom notices a mysterious stranger at the funeral of Paddy Dignam. *Now who is that lankylooking galoot over there in the macintosh?* (*U* 105) Hynes, the reporter, who is jotting down the names of the mourners, asks Bloom *do you know that fellow in the, fellow over there in the . . . Macintosh*, says Bloom and Hynes writes down the name *M'Intosh* (*U* 107–8), which then turns up in the *Evening Telegraph* (*U* 602). Later a *pedestrian in a brown macintosh* is glimpsed walking down Lower Mount Street in 'Wandering Rocks' (*U* 244) and we are told that he *loves a lady who is dead* (*U* 319). He also turns up at Burke's pub in 'Oxen of the Sun': *Golly, whatten tunket's you guy in the mackintosh?* (*U* 406). In the nightmare world of 'Circe' the man in the mackintosh accuses Bloom of being an imposter called Higgins (*U* 458) and in 'Ithaca' Bloom wonders *Who was M'Intosh?* as he goes to bed (*U* 681).

266 *JJ* 436.

267 *U* 53, 162, 163, 258, 259. See Eric Korn's essay 'Bloomsday, 1982' in *The Modern Movement: A TLS Companion*, ed John Goss (London: Harvill, 1992) pp.68–72.

268 *Imaging Ulysses: Richard Hamilton's Illustrations to James Joyce*. Exhibition at the British Museum, London, 2 February–19 May 2002.

269 *U* 72; the sketch is reproduced in *JJ* xxxvii (plate section).

270 *U* 621, 663.

271 *U* 317.

272 *U* 102.

273 *U* 225.

274 *U* 465, where Bloom is comically described as *a finished example of the new womanly man.*

275 *U* 370.

276 *U* 641.

277 Ibid.

278 *U* 317.

279 *U* 318.

280 *U* 327.

281 *U* 319.

282 *U* 687.

283 *U* 72.

284 *U* 728.

285 *U* 86.

286 *U* 21.

287 *U* 90, 98.

288 *U* 675.

289 *U* 93–8. Cunningham and Power are characters from 'Grace'.

290 *U* 119.

291 *U* 429.

292 *U* 141.

293 *U* 494.

294 *U* 539; 541.

295 *U* 548.

296 *U* 558.

297 *SL* 278.

298 *U* 626.

299 *U* 620. See also the conclusion of Joyce's essay 'James Clarence Mangan' (1902),

in which he states that the *high, original purpose* of literature is *the continual affirmation of the spirit* (*Occasional, Critical, and Political Writing*, p.60).

300 *U* 648.

301 Ibid.

302 *U* 655.

303 *U* 635.

304 *U* 689.

305 *SL* 285.

306 *U* 712.

307 *U* 722.

308 *U* 694.

309 *U* 731.

310 *U* 725–6; 729.

311 *U* 729.

312 *U* 723.

313 *U* 729.

314 Ibid.

315 *U* 731–2.

316 *JJ* 522. Did Joyce also have Dadaism in mind? According to Hans Richter, Dada meant 'da, da' (in Romanian): '"yes, yes" to life'. See *Dada: Art and Anti-Art*, p.31.

317 *JJ* 523–4.

318 Ezra Pound, *Guide to Kulcher* (Peter Owen, 1952), p.96.

319 Ezra Pound, *Selected Poems* (1975; repr. London: Faber and Faber, 1977), p.131: *Canto* XIV, one of the 'hell Cantos', in which the modern world is full of liars, idiots, usurers, 'the arse-belching of preachers', the envious and the corrupt.

320 *Occasional, Critical, and Political Writing*, p.28.

321 Ezra Pound, 'Paris Letter' to *The Dial* (June 1922) in *Literary Essays of Ezra Pound*, p. 408.

322 *JJ* 531.

323 T S Eliot, '*Ulysses*, Order and Myth' (1923) in *Selected Prose of T S Eliot*, ed Frank Kermode (1975; repr. London: Faber and Faber, 1984), p.175.

324 *The Question of Things Happening: The Letters of Virginia Woolf*, Volume II: 1912–1922, ed Nigel Nicolson (London: The Hogarth Press, 1976), p.551.

325 Anthony Cronin in 'The Master Builder', *The Modern Movement: A TLS Companion*, ed John Goss (London: Harvill, 1992), p.61.

326 *Bound and Gagged*, p.21.

327 Ibid., p.22.

328 *The Collected Essays, Journalism and Letters of George Orwell*, Volume I (London: Secker and Warburg, 1968), p.139.

329 *SL* 291.

330 *JJ* 509. There are several versions of what happened when Joyce met Proust. In one, Proust is said to have asked Joyce if he liked truffles. In another, they are supposed to have compared ailments. It is likely that Proust, who moved in elevated circles, mentioned several of his acquaintances, none of whom Joyce knew. He confided to a friend: *Proust would only talk about duchesses, while I was more concerned with their chambermaids*. (*JJ* 509) Other accounts suggest that Joyce was eager to have a serious conversation with Proust, but the ailing Frenchman (who died six months later) fled in horror from the tipsy Irishman.

331 *JJ* 537.

332 Evelyn Waugh, *Vile Bodies* (London: Penguin, 2000), pp.19–20.

333 *Bound and Gagged*, p.22.

334 Ibid., p.24. Home Office papers on *Ulysses* were to remain secret until 2037 under the 100-year rule, but in 1998 they were deposited without announcement in the vaults of the Public Record Office under Whitehall's 'Open Government' initiative. See the report in the *Guardian* (15 May 1998), pp.1, 3.

335 *SL* 285.

336 *Bound and Gagged*, p.24.

337 Ibid., p.25.

338 Ibid., p.28.

339 Ibid., pp.30–31.

340 *SL* 318. Joyce had already anticipated this in *Ulysses*. When Bloom starts to fall asleep his mind latches on to the phrase *Sinbad the Sailor*, but sound overtakes sense as he loses consciousness and we get *Tinbad the Tailor and Jinbad the Jailer and Whinbad the Whaler* and so on. (*U* 689)

341 *Selected Prose of T S Eliot*, pp.177–8.

342 *JJ* 716.

343 *JJ* 730.

344 *FW* 5. 9–10.

345 *FW* 380. 11–13.

346 *FW* 383.1. Thanks to Joyce, the word *quark* has entered modern physics, denoting 'any of a class of unobserved subatomic particles with a fractional electric charge, of which protons, neutrons, and other hadrons are thought to be composed' (*Concise Oxford Dictionary*).

347 *SL* 301–2. See *FW* 196–216, although the full name 'Anna Livia Plurabelle' does not appear in the text.

348 *JJ* 554.

349 *JJ* 546.

350 *JJ* 397.

351 *JJ* 186.

352 *JJ* 703.

353 *Nora*, p.434.

354 *FW* 121.15–16; 522.29–30.

355 *JJ* 546.

356 *JJ* 696.

357 *FW* 20.13–14.

358 *FW* 497.24–5.

359 *FW* 138.19–20. For instance, *the House of Blazes, the Parrot in Hell, the Orange Tree* and *the Glibt* are real Dublin pubs (*FW* 63.23–4), whereas *the Duck and Doggies, the Galloping Primrose* and the *All Swell That Aimswell* are Joyce's invention (*FW* 39.35–40.2).

360 *FW* 482.7.

361 *FW* 135.7.

362 *FW* 560.22–8.

363 *FW* 561.3–4.

364 *FW* 560.28.

365 *FW* 573.11.

366 *FW* 32.18–19; 535.34–5; 46.1; 3.3; 95.12.

367 *FW* 593.3.

368 *FW* 443.36–444.1–2.

369 *FW* 16.31–2.

370 *FW* 407.13–14.

371 *FW* 237.11.

372 *FW* 177.15–16, 23, 32.

373 *FW* 188.19;172.18–20.

374 *FW* 464.17; 467.25; 356.19–20; 284.21–2.

375 *FW* 190.36; 191.4.

376 *FW* 176.25–31.

377 *FW* 14.13–15.

378 *FW* 582.10; 167.4.

379 *FW* 216.3–4; 113.19; 398.29; 383.18.

380 *FW* 220.7–8.

381 *FW* 157.8; 107.6.

382 *FW* 526.23.

383 *FW* 431.15 96.13.

384 *FW* 431.29; 461.30–2.

385 *FW* 610.23–7.

386 *FW* 617.13–14; 620.12.

387 *FW* 104.1–2.

388 *FW* 3.6.

389 *FW* 34.18–19.

390 *SL* 388; and see *FW* 35ff, when Earwicker defends himself in Phoenix Park.

391 *FW* 35.6.

392 *FW* 32.14; 36.23–4.

393 *FW* 35.11; 36.33–4.

394 *FW* 35.20.

395 *FW* 421.23; 305.9.

396 *JJ* 722; from Gogarty's review of *Finnegans Wake* in the *Observer* (7 May 1939).

397 *FW* 424.32; 181.14–17. See also *U* 435, where Bloom is accused of being *A plagiarist. A soapy sneak masquerading as a litterateur.*

398 *FW* 424.35.

399 *FW* 152.18–19; 179.26–7.

400 *U* 82, *FW* 593.9; 479.36; *U* 732.

401 *FW* 614.5–12.

402 *FW* 6.9–10.

403 *FW* 4.15–16.

404 *FW* 627.23–4.

405 *FW* 58.19.

406 *P* 145.

407 *U* 34.

408 *FW* 614.32–3.

409 *JJ* 716.

410 There are ten thunderbolts, each containing 100 letters, except the last, which has 101. So there are 1001 letters in total, like *The Thousand and One Nights*, another important source for *Finnegans Wake*. See *FW* 3.15–17; 23.5–7;   44.20–21;   90.31–33; 113.9–11;   257.27–8;   314.8–9; 332.5–7; 414.19–20; 424.20–22.

411 *FW* 3.2; *SL* 314.

412 *P* 210. Joyce began 'The Day of the Rabblement' (1901) with a cryptic reference to *the Nolan* (Bruno was born near Nola): *No man, said the Nolan, can be a lover of the true or the good unless he abhors the multitude; and the artist, though he may employ the crowd, is very careful to isolate himself.* (*Occasional, Critical, and Political Writing*, p.50)

413 *FW* 180.4.

414 *FW* 482.1; 500.19; 415.17.

415 *FW* 536.34–5; 433.22–3.

416 Beckett, Samuel *et al*, *Our Exagmination round His Factification for Incamination of Work in Progress* (1929; repr. London: Faber and Faber, 1972), p.184.

417 *FW* 530.36; 238.21; 419.10–11.

418 *FW* 178.6–7.

419 *JJ* 703.

420 *FW* 120.12–14.

421 *FW* 388.3.

422 *FW* 231.14.

423 *FW* 5.3–4.

424 *FW* 324.20 See *JJ* 707.

425 *JJ* 703.

426 Ibid.

427 *JJ* 683.

428 *Independent Review* (8 May 2003).

429 *FW* 233.33.

430 William York Tindall, quoted in Bernard Benstock, *Joyce-again's Wake: An Analysis of Finnegans Wake* (Seattle: University of Washington Press, 1965), p.3.

431 *JJ* 598.

432 *SL* 323.

433 *JJ* 579.

434 *JJ* 584.

435 *JJ* 590.

436 *SL* 327.

437 *JJ* 557.

438 Anthony Burgess reviewing James Joyce, *Poems and Shorter Writings* (see List of Works) in the *Independent* (18 January 1991).

439 *JJ* 702.

440 *JJ* 700.

441 *FW* 173.33–6.

442 *The Joyce We Knew*, p.34.

443 Ibid. p.35.

444 Daniel Odier, *The Job: Interviews with William S Burroughs* (New York: Penguin, 1989), p.55.

445 Ibid. p.34. *The Joyce We Knew.*

446 Ibid. p.35.

447 *Our Exagmination . . .* , p.41.

448 Ibid. p.15; *FW* 188.14.

449 Ibid. p.14.

450 Quoted in James Knowlson, *Damned to Fame: The Life of Samuel Beckett* (London: Bloomsbury, 1996), p.101. When Beckett was stabbed by a Paris pimp in 1938, Joyce rushed to his bedside, paid for him to have a private room and lent him his favourite reading lamp. 'When I came to,' said Beckett, 'the first thing I remember was Joyce standing at the end of the ward and coming to see me.' (Ibid. p.282)

451 Ibid. p.160.

452 Ibid. p.290.

453 Stuart Gilbert, quoted in *Joyce's Lives,*

p.13.

454 *JJ* 699.

455 *Send him canorious, long to lung over us, high topseasoarious! Guard safe our Geoge!* See *Occasional, Critical, and Political Writing*, pp.212–5.

456 *JJ* 341.

457 *FW* 349.25.

458 *FW* 423.22–3.

459 *Nora*, pp.359–60.

460 *The Joyce We Knew*, p.55.

461 Ibid. p.57.

462 Robert McAlmon, 'Mr Joyce Directs an Irish Word Ballet', in *Our Exagmination . . .*, p.109.

463 James Joyce, quoted in *Joyce's Politics*, p.173.

464 *FW* 19.12–13.

465 *SL* 360.

466 See *PSW* 67. The second line in all editions reads *child*, but Joyce wrote this before he knew he had a grandson. Afterwards he changed *child* to *boy*.

467 *JJ* 645.

468 *JJ* 650.

469 *JJ* 662.

470 *FW* 522.34–5.

471 *JJ* 703.

472 *FW* 259.7–8.

473 Harold Nicolson, *Diaries and Letters 1930–1939*, ed Nigel Nicolson (London: Collins, 1966), pp.164–5.

474 *JJ* 667.

475 *Nora*, pp.392–3.

476 *JJ* 693.

477 *JJ* 712.

478 *FW* 627.34–628.2.

479 *JJ* 713.

480 *JJ* 721.

481 *SL* 369.

482 *JJ* 680.

483 *JJ* 731.

484 The James Joyce/Paul Léon Papers are now in the National Library of Ireland and were opened to the public in 1992. Léon was arrested in 1941 and mur-

dered by the Nazis in 1942.

485 *JJ* 741.

486 *Joyce-again's Wake*, p.122; *FW* 627.13–15.

487 *Nora*, p.453.

488 Ibid. p.454–5.

489 *JJ* 743.

490 *Damned to Fame*, p.105.

491 Rayner Heppenstall in 'Ulysses Returns', *The Modern Movement: A TLS Companion*, ed John Goss (London: Harvill, 1992) pp.63.

492 *Scotland On Sunday* (17 March 2002), 'Dublin leaves Joyce's literary legacy in ruins' by Nicola Byrne. Even in 1968, Joseph Strick's *Ulysses* was rejected by the Irish film censor's office. It was not passed for release in Ireland until 2001.

493 *F Scott Fitzgerald on Authorship*, ed Matthew J Broccoli (Columbia: University of South Carolina Press, 1996), p.91.

494 D J Taylor, 'Tales of the unexpected', *Guardian*, 28 July 2001.

495 *Damned to Fame*, p.352.

496 Jacques Derrida, 'Two Words for Joyce' in *Post Structuralist Joyce: Essays from the French*, ed Derek Attridge and Daniel Ferrer (Cambridge: Cambridge University Press, 1988), p.147. Derrida also describes his long essay 'Plato's Pharmacy' as 'a reading of *Finnegans Wake*'. See his *Dissemination*, translated by Barbara Johnson (Chicago: University of Chicago Press, 1981), p.88n20.

497 *JJ* 703.

498 Pierre Boulez, *Orientations* (London: Faber and Faber), pp.143–154.

499 Philip K Dick, *The Divine Invasion* (London: HarperCollins, 1996), p.15.

500 *P* 180–81.

Chronology

Year	Age	Life
1882		2 February: James Augustine Joyce born in Rathgar, a Dublin suburb.
1884	2	Family moves to Rathmines, Dublin. December: Brother Stanislaus born.
1887	5	Family moves to Bray, south of Kingstown (now Dun Loaghaire). John Joyce's uncle, William O'Connell, moves in with the family, as does Joyce's governess, Mrs 'Dante' Hearn Conway.
1888	6	Enrols at Clongowes Wood College, a Jesuit boys' day school near Sallins, County Kildare.
1891	9	Father loses job as Rates Collector. Joyce has to leave Clongowes. Writes 'Et Tu, Healy' in response to Parnell's death.
1892	10	Family moves to Blackrock.
1893	11	Enters Belvedere College, a Jesuit boys' day school.
1894	12	Family moves to Drumcondra. Wins the first of many essay competitions. Family moves to Dublin. Chooses Ulysses for the essay topic 'My Favourite Hero'.
1896	14	Claims to have begun his sexual life.
1898	16	Reads Ibsen; attends and reviews plays. Leaves Belvedere and enrols at University College Dublin.
1899	17	Attends W B Yeats's *The Countess Kathleen*; refuses to sign letter of protest against it in the *Freeman's Journal*.
1900	18	Reads 'Drama and Life' to the university's Literary and Historical Society. 'Ibsen's New Drama' published in the *Fortnightly Review*. Corresponds with Ibsen.
1901	19	Attacks the Irish Literary Theatre in 'The Day of the Rabblement'. Begins writing his 'epiphanies'.

Year	History	Culture
1882	Lord Frederick Cavendish and Thomas Burke are murdered in Phoenix Park.	Gabriele D'Annunzio, *Canto novo* and *Terra virgine*.
1884	Sir Henry Campbell-Bannerman becomes Chief Secretary for Ireland.	J K Huysmans, *À Rebours*. Henrik Ibsen, *The Wild Duck*.
1887	Arthur Balfour becomes Chief Secretary for Ireland. *The Times* publishes forged papers in which Parnell appears to condone the Phoenix Park Murders.	Arthur Conan Doyle, *A Study in Scarlet*. Thomas Hardy, *The Woodlanders*. Walter Pater, *Imaginary Portraits*. Émile Zola, *La terre*.
1888	Irish Plan of Campaign and boycotting denounced by Pope Leo XIII.	Édouard Dujardin, *Les Lauriers sont coupés*. Ibsen, *The Lady from the Sea*.
1891	Anti-Parnellite Irish National Federation founded in Dublin. Parnell loses three by-elections. 6 October: Parnell dies.	George Gissing, *New Grub Street*. Hardy, *Tess of the D'Urbervilles*. Oscar Wilde, *The Picture of Dorian Gray*
1892	Gladstone becomes Prime Minister after general election.	Italo Svevo, *Una Vita*. Ibsen, *The Master Builder*.
1893	Gladstone's second Home Rule Bill is passed by the Commons, but rejected by the Lords.	Stéphane Mallarmé, *Vers et prose*. Yeats, *The Celtic Twilight*.
1894	Gladstone resigns, succeeded by Lord Rosebery. The National Maternity Hospital, Holles Street, Dublin, opens. Dreyfus trial (1894–9) begins in Paris.	D'Annunzio, *Il trionfo della morte*. Ibsen, *Little Eyolf*. George Moore, *Esther Waters*. George Russell (AE), *Homeward: Songs by the Way*.
1896	John Dillon elected chairman of the anti-Parnellites.	Joseph Conrad, *An Outcast of the Islands*.
1898	William O'Brien founds the United Irish League at Westport to agitate for land reform. September: Queen Victoria visits Ireland.	D'Annunzio, *La città morta*. Svevo, *Senilità*. H G Wells, *The War of the Worlds*.
1899	Arthur Griffith founds *United Irishman*. Boer War begins.	Douglas Hyde, *Literary History of Ireland*. Ibsen, *When We Dead Awaken*. Irish Literary Theatre founded.
1900	The Irish Parliamentary Party (IPP) reunites ten years after it split; John Redmond is elected leader. Queen Victoria visits Ireland. Arthur Griffith founds Cumann na nGaedheal.	D'Annunzio, *Il fuoco*. Sigmund Freud, *The Interpretation of Dreams*. Jarry, *Ubu enchâiné*. Friedrich Nietzsche, *Ecce Homo*. Oscar Wilde dies.
1901	Queen Victoria dies; Edward VII accedes to the throne.	D'Annunzio, *Francesca da Rimini*. Anton Chekhov, *The Three Sisters*.

Year	Age	Life
1902	20	Brother George dies. Graduates from university; registers for Royal University Medical School, then leaves for Paris to study medicine. Back in Dublin for Christmas.
1903	21	In Paris again. Abandons medical school. April: Returns to Dublin due to mother's illness. August: Mother dies.
1904	22	Writes essay-story 'A Portrait of the Artist'. Begins *Stephen Hero*. Poems published, collected later as *Chamber Music*. Teaches at Clifton School, Dalkey. 16 June: First date with Nora Barnacle. Begins stories that will be collected in *Dubliners*. Writes 'The Holy Office'. Stays in the Martello tower, Sandycove, with Gogarty and Trench. October: Leaves Dublin with Nora, first to London, then Paris, Zurich, Trieste and Pola, where he teaches English at a Berlitz School.
1905	23	Moves with Nora to Trieste to teach English at another Berlitz School. 27 July: Son Giorgio born. His brother Stanislaus arrives in Trieste.
1906	24	Moves to Rome with Nora and Giorgio, where he works as a bank clerk. Begins 'The Dead'.
1907	25	The family returns to Trieste, where Joyce gives private English lessons. May: *Chamber Music* published by Elkin Mathews. 26 July: Daughter Lucia born. Beginnings of eye trouble. Reworks *Stephen Hero* as *A Portrait of the Artist as a Young Man*. Completes 'The Dead'.
1909	27	July: Visits Dublin with Giorgio. Signs contract with Maunsel & Co. for publication of *Dubliners*. Returns to Trieste (September), but goes back to Dublin (October) as cinema agent. December: Opens Ireland's first cinema, The Volta, in Mary Street.
1910	28	January: Returns to Trieste. The Volta Cinema fails. Maunsel & Co. postpone publication of *Dubliners*.
1912	30	May: Last trip to Ireland, visiting Dublin and Galway. Hopes of publishing *Dubliners* crushed. Writes 'Gas from a Burner'. Infatuation with Amalia Popper.
1914	32	February: *A Portrait of the Artist as a Young Man* begins serialization in the *Egoist*. June: *Dubliners* published by Grant Richards. August: Completes *Giacomo Joyce*. November: Begins *Ulysses*.

Year	History	Culture
1902	Treaty of Vereeniging ends Boer War. Arthur Balfour becomes Prime Minister. The Ulster Literary Theatre is founded in Belfast.	Conrad, *Heart of Darkness*. Conan Doyle, *The Hound of the Baskervilles*. Lady Gregory, *Cuchulain of Muirthemne* and, with Yeats, *Cathleen ni Houlihan*.
1903	The Irish Literary Theatre becomes the Irish National Theatre Society. St Patrick's Day declared a bank holiday.	Lady Gregory, *Poets and Dreamers*. Russell (AE), *The Divine Vision*. Shaw, *Man and Superman*.
1904	Arthur Griffith's *The Resurrection of Hungary: A Parallel for Ireland* appears in *United Irishman*. Anti-Jewish agitation in Limerick; Jews are 'insulted and assaulted' (*Irish Times*). Russo-Japanese War begins. Edward VII visits Ireland again. Lord Dunraven forms Irish Reform Association to campaign for devolution.	D'Annunzio, *Alcione* and *La figlia di Iorio*. Conrad, *Nostromo*. Russell (AE), *The Divine Vision*. J M Synge, *Riders to the Sea*. Symons, *Studies in Prose and Verse*. The Abbey Theatre opens with Yeats's *On Baile Strand* and Lady Gregory's *Spreading the News*.
1905	First issue of the *Irish Independent* newspaper. Ulster Unionist Council formed. George Wyndham resigns as chief secretary; James Bryce replaces him.	Conan Doyle, *The Return of Sherlock Holmes*. Moore, *The Lake*. J M Synge, *The Well of the Saints*. Wells, *Kipps*. Wilde, *De Profundis*.
1906	Liberal Party wins landslide majority in British general election. *Sinn Féin* appears, published and edited by Griffith.	John Galsworthy publishes *The Man of Property*, the first volume of the 'Forsyte Saga'. Beckett born.
1907	The Dungannon Clubs and Cumann na nGaedheal amalgamate to form the Sinn Féin League, which amalgamates with the National Council. Augustine Birrell becomes Chief Secretary for Ireland.	Padraic Colum, *Wild Earth*. Conrad, *The Secret Agent*. W H Davies, *Autobiography of a Super-Tramp*. Russell (AE), *Deirdre*. Synge, *The Playboy of the Western World*.
1909	Lord Lieutenant threatens to revoke the Abbey Theatre's patent if it stages a play by G B Shaw that has been refused a licence in England.	Ezra Pound, *Personae* and *Exultations*. Symons, *The Romantic Movement in English Poetry*. Synge, *The Tinker's Wedding* and *Poems and Translations*. Synge dies.
1910	Liberal government retains office in two British general elections.	E M Forster, *Howards End*. Freud, *On Psychoanalysis*. Yeats, *Poems II*.
1912	Unionists protest when Winston Churchill, a supporter of Home Rule, visits Belfast.	Conan Doyle, *The Lost World*. Franz Kafka writes *Metamorphosis*. Moore, *Salve*. James Stephens, *The Crock of Gold*.
1914	Third Home Rule Bill passed by the Commons, but altered by the Lords to exclude all Ulster permanently. It receives royal assent, but is suspended. Assassination of Archduke Ferdinand in Sarajevo. Austria-Hungary declares war on Serbia. Irish Volunteers smuggle guns into Ireland.	Moore, *Vale*. Pound, *Des Imagistes*. G B Shaw, *Pygmalion*. James Stephens, *Songs from the Clay* and *The Demi-Gods*. Yeats, *Responsibilities*. Wyndham Lewis and Pound found the Vorticist periodical *Blast*.

Year	Age	Life
1915	33	Stanislaus arrested and interned for remainder of the War. Joyce, Nora, Giorgio and Lucia leave Trieste for neutral Zurich. September: Serialization of *A Portrait of the Artist as a Young Man* in the *Egoist* comes to an end.
1916	34	Granted £100 from the British Civil List. *Dubliners* and *A Portrait of the Artist as a Young Man* published in United States by B W Heubsch.
1917	35	*A Portrait of the Artist as a Young Man* published in Britain by the Egoist Press. Eye trouble. Harriet Shaw Weaver becomes his (anonymous) patron. First three episodes of *Ulysses* completed, to be serialized in the *Egoist* and the *Little Review* the following year. First eye operation. Flirtation with Gertrude Kaempffer.
1918	36	*Exiles* published. Involvement in The English Players and altercation with Henry Carr and the British Consulate. More eye trouble.
1919	37	Issues of the *Little Review* confiscated and destroyed by US postal authorities. *Exiles* performed. Family returns to Trieste.
1920	38	Family moves to Paris. New York Society for the Prevention of Vice complains of the 'Nausicaa' issue of the *Little Review*.
1921	39	Editors of the *Little Review* convicted of publishing obscenity.
1922	40	2 February: *Ulysses* published in Paris by Shakespeare & Co. April: Nora and children visit Galway, Ireland, during the civil war. August: With Joyce, the family travels to England. Return to Paris in September.
1923	41	Begins *Work in Progress* (*Finnegans Wake*).
1924	42	Fragments of *Work in Progress* published in *transatlantic review*.
1927	45	Instalments of *Work in Progress* published in *transition*. First German translation of *Ulysses* (2nd translation: 1975). *Pomes Penyeach* published by Shakespeare & Co. Herbert Gorman's *James Joyce* (the first biography) published by B W Huebsch.
1928	46	*Anna Livia Plurabelle* published.
1929	47	*Tales Told of Shem and Shaun* published. *Ulysse*, the French translation of *Ulysses*, published. *Our Exagmination round his Factification for Incamination of Work in Progress* published by Shakespeare & Co.

Year	History	Culture
1915	William T Cosgrave (Sinn Féin) elected to Dublin city council. Supreme Council of IRB establishes a military committee and collaborates with Irish Volunteers to plan an uprising.	Rupert Brooke, *1914 and Other Poems*. D H Lawrence, *The Rainbow*. Virginia Woolf, *The Voyage Out*.
1916	The Easter Rising in Dublin with about 1,000 Irish Volunteers and 200 Citizen Army. Lord Lieutenant declares martial law.	Guillaume Apollinaire, *Le poète assassiné*. Yeats, *Reveries over Childhood and Youth*.
1917	Revolution in Russia. USA declares war on Germany and enters the First World War. Éamon de Valera wins by-election for Sinn Féin; more victories follow.	Apollinaire, *Les Mamelles de Tirésias*. T S Eliot, *Prufrock and Other Observations*. Ezra Pound, *Homage to Sextus Propertius*. Stephens, *Reincarnation*. Yeats, *The Wild Swans at Coole*.
1918	Military Service Act threatens conscription for Ireland: there is a one-day general strike in protest (except in Ulster).	Wyndham Lewis, *Tarr*. Russell (AE), *The Candle of Vision*.
1919	Two members of Royal Irish Constabulary shot dead by Irish Volunteers: regarded as first incident in the 'War of Independence'.	Franz Kafka, *In the Penal Colony* and *A Country Doctor*. Marcel Proust, *Within a Budding Grove*.
1920	First meeting of League of Nations. Sinn Féin takes control of most borough and urban councils in local elections.	T S Eliot, *The Sacred Wood*. Lady Gregory, *Visions and Beliefs in the West of Ireland*.
1921	Martial law extended to counties Clare, Kilkenny, Waterford and Wexford.	D'Annunzio, *Notturno*. André Breton, *Les Champs magnétiques*.
1922	Anglo-Irish Treaty narrowly approved by Dáil Eireann. Griffith succeeds de Valera as President. Provisional Free State government takes over from British administration.	Colum, *Dramatic Legends and Other Poems*. T S Eliot, *The Waste Land*. Lawrence, *Aaron's Rod*. Russell (AE), *The Interpreters*. Proust dies.
1923	William Cosgrave founds Cumann na nGaedheal as pro-Treaty party.	Sean O'Casey, *The Shadow of a Gunman*.
1924	Mutiny in Free State army signals end of IRB. De Valera expelled from Northern Ireland.	Oliver St John Gogarty, *An Offering of Swans*. O'Casey, *Juno and the Paycock*.
1927	Irish Free State general election: de Valera and Fianna Fáil enter the Dáil as largest opposition party. Cumann na nGaedheal still the largest party in the Dáil. Ireland's first automatic telephone exchange opens in Dublin.	Colum, *The Roads Round Ireland*. Kafka, *Amerika*. Wyndham Lewis, *Time and Western Man*. Proust, *Time Regained*. Woolf, *To the Lighthouse*.
1928	James McNeill becomes Governor-General of the Free State.	Lawrence, *Lady Chatterley's Lover*. Wyndham Lewis, *The Childermass*.
1929	The Censorship of Publications Act sets up the Irish Censorship Board; information on contraception is classified as 'indecent literature'.	Samuel Beckett's first short story, 'Assumption', appears in *transition*. Jean Cocteau, *Les enfants terribles*.

Year	Age	Life
1930	48	*Haveth Childers Everywhere* published. Stuart Gilbert's *James Joyce's Ulysses* published. Joyce becomes enthusiastic champion of John Sullivan, the Irish tenor.
1931	49	4 July: Joyce and Nora married in London. 29 December: Father dies.
1932	50	15 February: Grandson Stephen James born. Writes 'Ecce Puer'. Lucia has a breakdown and stays in a clinic. Revised edition of *Ulysses* published. Paul Léon increasingly works with Joyce.
1933	51	Lucia hospitalized. 6 December: Judge John M Woolsey's momentous decision: ban lifted on publication of *Ulysses* in United States. Odyssey Press edition of *Ulysses*.
1934	52	*Ulysses* published in United States. Lucia hospitalized again. *The Mime of Mick Nick and the Maggies* published.
1936	54	*Ulysses* published in Britain by John Lane, The Bodley Head. *Collected Poems* published in New York. *A Chaucer ABC*, with illuminated initial letters by Lucia Joyce, published in Paris.
1937	55	*Storyella She is Syung* is the last *Work in Progress* fragment to be published.
1939	57	*Finnegans Wake* published. Family leaves Paris for Saint-Gérand-le-Puy, near Vichy.
1940	58	Family moves to Zurich. They are obliged to leave Lucia in Occupied France.
1941		13 January: Joyce dies after surgery on a perforated ulcer. Buried in Fluntern Cemetery, Zurich.

Year	History	Culture
1930	Irish Free State elected to council of League of Nations. Extreme parties (Communist and Nazi) win German elections: no majority to form a government.	W H Auden, *Poems*. Beckett, 'Whoroscope'. Colum, *Old Pastures*. T S Eliot, *Ash Wednesday*. Wyndham Lewis, *The Apes of God*.
1931	First edition of De Valera's *Irish Press* newspaper in Dublin, a platform for Fianna Fáil.	Beckett, *Proust*. Wyndham Lewis, *Hitler*.
1932	Army Comrades Association formed (later the National Guard, nicknamed 'Blueshirts'). Fianna Fáil wins general election; de Valera succeeds Cosgrave as President of Executive Council.	Auden, *The Orators*. Beckett, 'Sedendo et Quiescendo', 'Text' and 'Home Olga'. Frank O'Connor, *The Wild Bird's Nest*. Seán O'Faoláin, *Midsummer Night Madness*.
1933	Fianna Fáil wins general election. Oath of allegiance removed from Irish constitution. Cumann na nGaedheal, National Guard and Centre Party merge to form Fine Gael. First air service from Ireland to Britain.	O'Casey, *Within the Gates*. O'Faoláin, *A Nest of Simple Folk*. George Orwell, *Down and Out in Paris and London*. Raymond Queneau, *Le Chiendent*.
1934	Dollfuss, Austrian Chancellor, murdered by Nazis. Death of Hindenberg: Hitler assumes power.	Beckett, *More Pricks than Kicks*. Wyndham Lewis, *Men without Art*. O'Casey, *The Flying Wasp*.
1936	George V dies; Edward VIII accedes to throne, but abdicates in December. George VI accedes to the throne. Irish Free State creates Aer Lingus as national airline.	Auden, *The Ascent of F6*. Daphne du Maurier, *Jamaica Inn*. Gogarty, *As I Was Going Down Sackville Street*.
1937	Fianna Fáil wins general election; Eamon de Valera becomes Taoiseach and Minister for External Affairs.	Auden, *Letters from Iceland*. O'Flaherty, *Famine*. Wyndham Lewis, *Blasting and Bombardiering*.
1939	IRA bombing campaign in Britain begins. Britain recognizes Franco's government in Spain. Germany invades Poland.	Raymond Chandler, *The Big Sleep*. Wyndham Lewis, *The Hitler Cult and How It Will End*. Yeats dies.
1940	Emergency anti-IRA legislation introduced in Irish Free State. Germany invades Denmark and Norway, then Low Countries and France.	Chandler, *Farewell, My Lovely*. Greene, *The Power and the Glory*. Hemingway, *For Whom the Bell Tolls*.
1941	US Lend-Lease Bill signed by Roosevelt. Rommel opens attack in North Africa. Belfast devastated by air raids. Éire fire brigades (from Dublin and Dun Laoghaire) give assistance. German bombs fall on North Strand, Dublin, and elsewhere. German battleship, *Bismarck*, sunk. Clothes rationing in Britain. Germany attacks Russia. Soviet Government leaves Moscow. Sinking of HMS *Ark Royal*. German attack on Moscow halted. Japanese attack on Pearl Harbor. United States enters the Second World War. In Ireland, outbreak of foot-and-mouth disease kills 40,000 cattle.	Auden, *New Year Letter*. Churchill, *Into Battle*. Vladimir Nabokov, *The Real Life of Sebastian Knight*. Kate O'Brien's novel *The Land of Spices* banned by the Irish Free State Board of Censors.

List of Works

The Cat and the Devil, illustrated by Gerald Rose (London: Faber and Faber, 1965); illustrated by Roger Blachon with an Introduction by Stephen James Joyce (London: Moonlight Publishing, 1980). This short story began as a letter (10 August 1936) from Joyce to his grandson. The Devil is a caricature of Joyce and *has a strong Irish accent.*

Chamber Music (1907; repr. London: Jonathan Cape, 1980)

The Critical Writings of James Joyce, ed Ellsworth Mason and Richard Ellmann (1959; repr. London: Faber and Faber 1989, 1993)

Dubliners (1914; repr. Oxford: Oxford University Press, 2000, ed Jeri Johnson)

Exiles: A Play in Three Acts (1918; repr. with Joyce's notes and an Introduction by Padraic Colum, London: Jonathan Cape, 1952)

Finnegans Wake (1939; repr. London: Faber and Faber, 1960)

Giacomo Joyce (1968; repr. London: Faber and Faber, 1984, ed Richard Ellmann)

Occasional, Critical, and Political Writing, ed Kevin Barry (Oxford: Oxford University Press, 2000)

Poems and Shorter Writings, ed Richard Ellmann, A Walton Litz and John Whittier-Ferguson (1991; repr. London: Faber and Faber, 2001)

Pomes Penyeach (1927; repr. London: Faber and Faber, 1968)

A Portrait of the Artist as a Young Man (1916; repr. Oxford: Oxford

University Press, 2000, ed Jeri Johnson)
Selected Letters of James Joyce, ed Richard Ellmann (1975; repr. London: Faber and Faber, 1992)

Stephen Hero, ed Theodore Spencer (1944; rev. edn. St Albans: Triad/Panther, 1977, eds John J Slocum and Herbert Cahoon)

Ulysses (1922; repr. Oxford: Oxford University Press, 1998, ed Jeri Johnson). The 1922 first edition of *Ulysses* contains errors and misprints (due essentially to the the French printer's lack of English), but successive editions have only corrupted it further, culminating in the so-called 'corrected text' edited by Hans Walter Gabler (1984; repr. London: The Bodley Head, 1986), which, after an enthusiastic reception, has over the years received considerable criticism. In the end, the 1922 edition remains the least faulty text and the one closest to Joyce's original intentions. Nevertheless, interested readers might like to seek out the three-volume *Ulysses, A Critical and Synoptic Edition*, prepared by Hans Walter Gabler with Wolfhard Steppe and Claus Melchion (New York, London: Garland, 1984), the reading text of which led to the 1986 'corrected text'.

Letters of James Joyce, eds Stuart Gilbert (Vol I, London: Faber and Faber, 1957) and Richard Ellmann (Vols II and III, London: Faber and Faber, 1966).

Further Reading

As might be imagined, there is a vast amount of secondary literature on the life and art of James Joyce. The following books are a good place to start.

BOOKS

Attridge, Derek, *The Cambridge Companion to James Joyce* (Cambridge: Cambridge University Press, 1990)

——————— and Ferrer, Daniel, eds, *Post-structuralist Joyce: Essays from the French* (Cambridge: Cambridge University Press, 1984)

Beckett, Samuel *et al*, *Our Exagmination round his Factification for Incamination of Work in Progress* (1929; repr. London: Faber and Faber, 1972)

Benstock, Bernard, *Joyce-again's Wake: An Analysis of Finnegans Wake* (Seattle: University of Washington Press, 1965). One of the better books on *Finnegans Wake*.

Bishop, John, *Joyce's Book of the Dark* (Madison, Wisconsin: University of Wisconsin, 1986). A modern look at *Finnegans Wake*.

Blamires, Harry, *The Bloomsday Book* (1966; repr. London: Methuen, 1985). A page-by-page guide to *Ulysses* for the student or general reader.

Budgen, Frank, *James Joyce and the Making of 'Ulysses'* (1934; repr. London: Oxford University Press, 1972).

Campbell, Joseph, and Robinson, Henry Morton, eds, *A Skeleton Key to Finnegans Wake* (London: Faber and Faber, 1947)

Deane, Seamus, *Celtic Revivals* (1985; repr. London: Faber and Faber, 1987). Contains three excellent essays 'Joyce and Stephen: the Provincial Intellectual', 'Joyce and Nationalism' and 'Joyce and Beckett'.

Deming, Robert H, ed, *James Joyce: The Critical Heritage* (2 vols; London: Routledge & Kegan Paul, 1970)

Eco, Umberto, *The Aesthetics of Chaosmos: The Middle Ages of James Joyce*, trans Ellen Esrock (1982; repr. Massachusetts: Harvard University Press, 1989). A fascinating study of Joyce's aesthetic programme. Joyce regarded himself as *Steeled in the school of old Aquinas* ('The Holy Office') and Eco argues that 'Joyce was the node where the Middle Ages and the avant-garde meet.'

Eliot, T S, '*Ulysses*, Order and Myth', *The Dial* (Nov. 1923), repr. in Frank Kermode, ed, *Selected Prose of T S Eliot* (1975; repr. London: Faber and Faber, 1984, pp.175–8). Dated, but still one of the best introductions to *Ulysses* ever written.

Ellmann, Richard, *James Joyce* (1959; rev. edn. Oxford: Oxford University Press, 1983). Monumental and indispensable, but not without its critics (see McGinley).

——————, *Ulysses on the Liffey* (1972; repr. London: Faber and Faber, 1984). Ellmann delves deep into the structure and themes of *Ulysses*. A fascinating interpretation by a great Joyce scholar.

Jackson, John Wyse, and Costello, Peter, *John Stanislaus Joyce: The Voluminous Life and Genius of James Joyce's Father* (London: Fourth Estate, 1997). A vivid portrait: Joyce's fiction was 'an imaginative recreation not of his own life but of his father's'.

Joyce, James, *A Shorter Finnegans Wake*, ed Anthony Burgess (1966; repr. London: Faber and Faber, 1988). A good introduction to *Finnegans Wake* for anyone intimidated by the size of the original, with useful link passages by Burgess.

Joyce, Stanislaus, *My Brother's Keeper: James Joyce's Early Years*, ed, Richard Ellmann (London: Faber and Faber, 1958). Younger brother with a few scores to settle.

Levin, Harry, *James Joyce: A Critical Introduction* (Norfolk, Connecticut: New Directions Books, 1941).

——————, ed, *The Essential James Joyce* (1948; repr. London: Triad Paladin, 1985). A selection of Joyce's works that covers his entire writing life, with useful introductory notes.

Maddox, Brenda, *Nora: A Biography of Nora Joyce* (1988; repr. London: Minerva, 1990). Joyce's 'companion' laid bare and the perfect companion to Ellmann's biography.

Manganiello, Dominic, *Joyce's Politics* (Routledge & Kegan Paul, 1980). Written 'to dispel the view that Joyce had no politics', this book places Joyce in the context of Irish history and politics and persuaded Ellmann to revise his biography.

McGinley, Bernard, *Joyce's Lives: Uses and Abuses of the Biografiend* (London: University of North London Press, 1996). McGinley takes on Ellmann and Joyce's other biographers in this entertaining study.

Nabokov, Vladimir, *Lectures on Literature*, ed Fredson Bowers (1980; repr. London: Picador, 1983). Contains Nabokov's fine lecture on *Ulysses*, taking us episode-by-episode through the novel.

O'Connor, Ulick, ed, *The Joyce We Knew* (Cork: The Mercier Press, 1967): Joyce recollected in tranquillity (and with hindsight) by four of his Dublin friends.

AUDIO

The Spoken Word – Writers: Historic Recordings from the British Library Sound Archive (London: British Library Publishing Division, 2003). Includes Joyce reciting (not reading) 'Anna Livia Plurabelle' from *Finnegans Wake*.

FILMS

Passages from Finnegans Wake (Mary Ellen Bute, 1965)
With Ray Flanagan (Young Shem), Peter Haskell (Shem), Page Johnson (Shaun), Martin J Kelley (Finnegan) and Jane Reilly (Anna Livia).

Ulysses (Joseph Strick, 1967)
With Milo O'Shea (Leopold Bloom), Barbara Jefford (Molly Bloom), Maurice Roëves (Stephen Dedalus) and T P McKenna (Buck Mulligan).

A Portrait of the Artist as a Young Man (Joseph Strick, 1979)
With Bosco Hogan (Stephen Dedalus), T P McKenna (Simon Dedalus) and Sir John Gielgud (The Preacher).

James Joyce's Women (Michael Pearce, 1985)
With Fionnula Flanagan (Nora Joyce, Gertie MacDowell, Harriet Shaw Weaver, Main Washerwoman and Molly Bloom), Chris O'Neill (James Joyce), Tony Lyons (Leopold Bloom), Paddy Dawson (Stanislaus Joyce) and Martin Dempsey (John Joyce).

The Dead (John Huston, 1987)
With Angelica Huston (Gretta Conroy) and Donal McCann (Gabriel Conroy).

Nora (Pat Murphy, 1999)
With Ewan McGregor (James Joyce) and Susan Lynch (Nora Barnacle).

A Shout from the Streets (Fred DeVecca, 2000)
A short film inspired by James Joyce's *Ulysses*. Starring Stephen Adams, Doug Creighton, Bridget Kirsten MacAirt and Daniel Popowich.

Pitch 'n' Putt with Beckett and Joyce (Donald Clarke, 2001)
With Martin Murphy (James Joyce) and Arthur Riordan (Samuel Beckett).

bl,.m (Sean Walsh, 2003)
With Stephen Rea (Leopold Bloom), Angeline Ball (Molly Bloom) and

Hugh O'Conor (Stephen Dedalus).

James Joyce's Ulysses (LWT, 1988)
Combines drama and documentary. Starring David Suchet, T P
McKenna and Sorcha Cusack.

Ulysses (BBC, 2001)
Documentary narrated by poet and critic Tom Paulin.

MUSIC

Finnegans Wake inspired several works by the American composer John
Cage (1912–92):
'The Wonderful Widow of Eighteen Springs' (1942). A song adapted
from the 'Isobel' passage.
Roaratorio: An Irish Circus on Finnegans Wake (1979). A long chaotic work
incorporating phrases from the *Wake* into a tapestry of noise, voice, song
and traditional Irish music.
Writing for the Second Time through Finnegans Wake (1979). The 'libretto'
of *Roaratorio*, spoken by Cage.
Marcel Duchamp, James Joyce, Eric Satie: An Alphabet (1982). A radio play
featuring James Joyce as a character.
'Nowth Upon Nacht' (1984). A song with lyrics adapted from *Finnegans
Wake*.

Acknowledgements

Extracts from all of James Joyce's works, including exceptionally a number of letters, reproduced with the permission of his Estate; © Copyright Estate of James Joyce. My thanks to Barbara Schwepcke for suggesting this book in the first place, to Robert Pritchard and Sarah Barlow for helping it along, to Gary Baker for reading the manuscript and arguing with me about Joyce, to Phil Baker and Claudia Pugh-Thomas for some useful exchanges and to Claire Faherty at Oughterard Tourism & Development for answering my questions. Finally, this book would not have been possible without the love and support of Ali, who foolishly agreed to be my wife during its composition.

Picture Sources

The author and publishers wish to express their thanks to the following sources of illustrative material and/or permission to reproduce it. They will make proper acknowledgements in future editions in the event that any omissions have occurred.

AKG Images (London); pp.13. British Museum: pp, 41,85. Beinecke Rare Book and Manuscript Library, Yale University: pp. 3, 30, 40, 75, 97, 100, 125, 126, 133. Chester G Anderson: pp 48 Croessmann Collection. University of Southern Illinois Library Carbondale: pp.2, 18, 28, 36, 135. Getty Images:pp 139. Giornalfoto, Trieste: pp 55. Irish Times: pp 44. Jane Lidderdale: pp 69. Lawrence Collection, National Library of Ireland: pp.9, 51. Lebrecht Picture Library: pp. iii, 82, 131. Poetry, Rare Books Collection, University Libraries, State University of New York, Buffalo: pp. 1, 71, 78, 99. Courtesy Richard Hamilton, Gagosian Gallery (DACS): pp. 89.Topham Picturepoint: pp. 25 Scala Art Resource: pp. 38

Index

Freud, Sigmund, 79, 103–4, 127
'From a Banned Writer to a Banned Singer', 122

Gaelic League, 19, 21
Galway, 39, 57, 61, 64, 98–9
Garnett, Edward, 72
'Gas from a Burner', 6, 66
George V, King, 63
Germany, 76
Giacomo Joyce, 67, 70–1
Gide, André, 84
Gilbert, Stuart, 121, 123
Gladstone, W E, 5, 7
Gogarty, Oliver St John, 34–5, 37, 42, 49; as Mulligan, 34, 45, 70; Martello Tower episode, 43–5; Joyce snubs, 59–60; plot against Joyce, 61; on *Finnegans Wake*, 113
Gorman, Herbert, 123
Gregory, Lady, 28, 42
Guinness, Sir Noah, 108

Hamilton, Richard, 88
Healy, Michael, 72
Healy, Tim, 7, 110
Heap, Jane, 83
Hebrew, 90
Hemingway, Ernest, 84
Hitler, Adolf, 130
'Holy Office, The', 42–3, 49, 50
Home Office, 98, 101–2, 129
Home Rule, 4, 6, 55
Homer, 10; *Odyssey*, 11, 52, 78, 87, 90, 93, 95, 133
Huebsch, B W, 73, 84
Huelsenbeck, Richard, 72
Humpty Dumpty, 114

Hunter, Alfred, 39, 52
Hyde, Douglas, 19

Ibsen, Henrik, 15–16, 21–3, 25, 26, 37; *When We Dead Awaken*, 22
Il Piccolo della Sera, 55–6, 59, 64, 68
Imagist verse, 41, 68
International Joyce Foundation, 136
Invincibles, 4
Ireland, viii–xi, 53, 66, 134; anti-Semitism, 90; cattle embargo, 64; civil war, 98–9; in *Finnegans Wake*, 108, 115; independence, 131; Joyce and, 8, 25, 40, 49, 51, 62, 79; politics, 54, 55–6, 79; tourist industry, 136; *see also* Easter Rising; Home Rule
Irish, xi, 7–8, 62, 89, 104
Irish Free State, ix, 4, 25, 99, 115, 124, 125
Irish Homestead, 27, 41–2
Irish language, 19, 90
Irish Literary Theatre, 25
Irish Parliamentary Party (IPP), 6, 7
Irish Republican Army (IRA), 55, 99
Irish Republican Brotherhood (IRB), 55, 79
Irish Revival, 20, 21, 25, 28, 30, 42, 43
Irish Statesman, 27
Italian, 48, 106
Italy, 41, 54
Ivry, 127

James, Henry, viii
James, William, 32
Jesuits, 5, 6
Jews, xi, 52, 89

assessments of *Ulysses* and *Finnegans Wake*, 107; literary borrowings, 113; strain of writing *Finnegans Wake*, 118–19; preoccupation with Dublin, 119–20, 124; personality, 121–2; attempts to help John Sullivan, 122; marriage, 123; self-publicity, 123; concern over Lucia, 125–7; and psychoanalysis, 127; illness, 127, 132, 134; and Second World War, 130–2; death and funeral, 134

Joyce, John Stanislaus ('Stannie'), 26, 53, 65; early years, 3, 11–12, 17; diary, 14, 37, 44; and mother's death, 33; praises *Stephen Hero*, 48; in Trieste, 50, 55, 57, 63, 66, 79, 81; arrested and interned, 70–1; cooled relations with brother, 79; reaction to *Ulysses*, 80; sings 'Finnegan's Wake', 104–5; in *Finnegans Wake*, 109; on *Work in Progress*, 118

Joyce, John Stanislaus: work, 1, 8, 107; as Simon Dedalus, 2; 'character', 2–3; anticlericalism, 7; belief in James's future, 10, 57; temper, 17; reads Ibsen, 21; and George's death, 26; encourages James to leave Dublin, 27; and May's death, 33; disapproval of James's elopement, 57, 60; pleasure in grandson, 60; Nora and children visit, 98; attacked in Phoenix Park, 112; death, 124

Joyce, Lucia, 57, 64, 75, 133, 135; visits Galway during civil war, 98–9; legitimized by Joyce's mar-

riage, 123; mental instability, 125–7; death, 127

Joyce, Mabel Josephine Anne ('Baby'), 4, 37

Joyce, Margaret Alice ('Poppie'), 3, 33

Joyce, Mary Jane (May), 3–4; portrait, 3; reads Ibsen, 21; and George's death, 26; deteriorating health, 32; death, 33

Joyce, Mary Kathleen, 3–4

Joyce, Stephen James, 99, 125, 133

Judaism, 59

Jung, Carl, 74, 79, 104, 126; on *Finnegans Wake*, 131

Kaempffer, Gertrude, 74

Kettle, Thomas, 19, 53, 60, 131

La Fontaine, Jean de, 110

Lamb, Charles, 52; *The Adventures of Ulysses*, 10, 52, 93, 95

Lane, John, 128

Larbaud, Valéry, 84–5

'Lass of Aughrim, The', 54

Lawrence, D H, xi; *The Rainbow*, 72

Leavis, F R, 102

Leiris, Michel, 106

Leitrim, 4

Léon, Paul, 132

Leslie, Shane, 98

Lessing, Doris, ix

Lewis, Wyndham, 41, 82, 130

Liffey, River, 11, 95, 105, 107, 108, 114, 120, 129

Linati, Carlo, 83

literature, 20, 26, 30, 89; English, ix, 21, 98, 134; European, 14, 37; for-

Stein, Gertrude, 106
Stendhal, 14
Stephen Hero, 21, 26, 37, 41, 44, 47–8, 52, 57
Stephens, James, 118
Stramm, August, 106
stream of consciousness, 32, 58, 70, 137
Sullivan, John, 122
Surrealism, 72, 106
Svevo, Italo, *see* Schmitz, Ettore
Swift, Jonathan, 111; as Isaac Bickerstaff, 108
Symbolism, 21, 31
Symons, Arthur, 29, 47, 53
Synge, J M, 25, 30, 42
Syracuse, 57

Taylor, D J, 136
Thom's Official Directory, 66
Time magazine, 128
Times, The, 6
Tone, Theobald Wolfe, 8
transatlantic review, 69, 105
transition, 69, 105
Trench, Samuel Chevenix, 43–5; as Haines, 45
Trieste, 47, 49–50, 55, 62–4, 66–7, 70–1, 79, 81; composition of *Ulysses*, x, 87; Scuola Superiore di Commercio Revoltella, 66; Università del Popolo, 56
Trinity College, 34
Tristan and Isolde, 110, 111
Tzara, Tristan, 72

Ulysses, 10–11, 52, 87, 89, 92, 93, 95

Ulysses, 23, 53, 67, 81, 87–96, 103, 124, 138; *AEIOU* joke, 27; 'Aeolus', 61; bawdy songs, 34; borrowings in *Finnegans Wake*, 113; censorship in Britain, 101–2; 'Circe', 62, 78, 83, 92; composition, 70, 72, 73, 76–8, 80–1, 83; Cranly, 19; 'Cyclops', 52, 78–9; date of action, 39, 87; Donovan, 19; and *Dubliners*, 52–3, 83; episodes, 88; 'Eumaeus', 58, 83, 93; Gerty McDowell, 74, 77, 79; H Rumbold, 76; Haines, 45; 'Ithaca', 61, 85, 94, 137; John Eglington, 18; Kevin Egan, 31; Leopold Bloom, 12, 59, 60, 67, 74, 87–96, 116; 'Lotus Eaters', 77, 94; Lynch, 19; McGann, 19; Madden and Davin, 19; Molly Bloom, 87, 90–1, 95–6; Mulligan, 34, 45, 70, 89; 'Nausicaa', 77, 79, 83; 'Nestor', 38; nighttown, 12; 'Oxen of the Sun', 59, 80–1; 'Penelope', 84, 95, 101, 137; Phoenix Park Murders, 4, 93; plot, 87; proof corrections, 84; publication, 83–6, 128–9; reception, 97–8, 103; Richie Goulding, 45; Sandymount Strand, 15, 31, 79; 'Scylla and Charybdis', 18; serialization, 74, 76; Simon Dedalus, 2; 'Sirens', 52, 77, 78; Stephen Dedalus, viii, 33, 64, 70, 79, 87, 88–9, 92–5, 114; stream of consciousness, 32, 70; summary, 83; Telemachia, 74; 'Telemachus', 91; 'Tower episode', 44–5; US ban and trial, 84, 128
unconscious, collective, 104, 108

LIFE & TIMES FROM HAUS

Churchill
by Sebastian Haffner
'One of the most brilliant things of
any length ever written about
Churchill.' *TLS*
1-904341-07-1 (pb) £8.99
1-904341-06-3 (hb) £12.99

Dietrich
by Malene Skaerved
'It is probably the best book ever on
Marlene.' C. Downes
1-904341-13-6 (pb) £8.99
1-904341-12-8 (hb) £12.99

Beethoven
by Martin Geck
'. . . this little gem is a truly handy
reference.' *Musical Opinion*
1-904341-00-4 (pb) £8.99
1-904341-03-9 (hb) £12.99

Prokofiev
by Thomas Schipperges
'beautifully made, . . . well-produced
photographs, . . . with useful
historical nuggets.' *The Guardian*
1-904341-32-2 (pb) £8.99
1-904341-34-9 (hb) £12.99

Curie
by Sarah Dry
'. . . this book could hardly be bettered'
New Scientist
selected as **Outstanding Academic Title**
by *Choice*
1-904341-29-2 (pb) £8.99

Einstein
by Peter D Smith
'Concise, complete, well-produced and
lively throughout, . . . a bargain at the
price.' *New Scientist*
1-904341-15-2 (pb) £8.99
1-904341-14-4 (hb) £12.99

Casement
by Angus Mitchell
'hot topic' *The Irish Times*
1-904341-41-1 (pb) £8.99

Britten
by David Matthews
'I have read them all – but none with as
much enjoyment as this.' *Literary Review*
1-904341-21-7 (pb) £8.99
1-904341-39-X (hb) £12.99

De Gaulle
by Julian Jackson
'this concise and distinguished book'
Andrew Roberts *Sunday Telegraph*
1-904341-44-6 (pb) £8.99

Orwell
by Scott Lucas
'short but controversial assessment . . .
is sure to raise a few eyebrows' *Sunday
Tasmanian*
1-904341-33-0 (pb) £8.99

Bach
by Martin Geck
'The production values of the book are
exquisite, too.'
The Guardian
1-904341-16-0 (pb) £8.99
1-904341-35-7 (hb) £12.99

Kafka
by Klaus Wagenbach
'One of the most useful books about Kafka
ever published' *Frankfurter Allgemeine
Zeitung*
1-904341-02 -0 (PB) £8.99
1-904341-01-2 (hb) £12.99

Dostoevsky
by Richard Freeborn
'. . . wonderful . . . a learned guide'
The Sunday Times
1-904341-27-6 (pb) £8.99

Brahms
by Hans Neunzig
'readable, comprehensive and
attractively priced'
The Irish Times
1-904341-17-9 (pb) £8.99

Verdi
by Barbara Meier
'These handy volumes fill a gap in the
market . . . admirably.' *Classic fM*
1-904341-21-7 (pb) £8.99
1-904341-39-X (hb) L12.99

Armstrong
by David Bradbury
'generously illustrated . . . a fine and well-
researched introduction' George Melly
Daily Mail
1-904341-46-2 (pb) £8.99
1-904341-47-0 (hb) £12.99